prima

the quick and easy
cookbook

over 250 recipes

Book Acknowledgements

Photographers
Jean Cazals, David Brittan, Pete Cassidy, Hugh Johnson,
Sam Stowell, Stephen Conroy, Sean Myers, Tim Winter,
Martin Brigdale, Richard Kolker, Juliette Piddington

Acknowledgements
I would like to thank Amy Minden, Kate Titford, Heather Mairs,
Kim Morphew and Laura Anthony for their contribution and
help with the book.

THIS IS A CARLTON BOOK

Text and photographs copyright © 2002
The National Magazines Company Limited
Design copyright © 2002 Carlton Books Limited

This edition published by
Carlton Books Limited 2002
20 Mortimer Street
London W1T 3JW

Editorial Manager: **Judith More**
Art Director: **Penny Stock**
Executive Editor: **Zia Mattocks**
Design: **Cobalt Information Design**
Editors: **Lisa Dyer** and **Jo Lethaby**
Production Controller: **Janette Burgin**

prima

the quick and easy
cookbook

over 250 recipes

katie rogers

CARLTON

contents

introduction

With people leading such busy lives and having such different lifestyles, it is difficult to come up with a cookery book that caters for everyone's needs, but that is what we've aimed to do here. As well as 250 easy-to-prepare recipes, including lots of ideas for quick after-work suppers, advice and tips are given on how to stock your cupboards, fridge and freezer, and guidelines are provided for buying and cooking basic ingredients.

If you really want to save time in the kitchen, the first step is to sort out your cupboards with our chapter 'The Basics' (page 8). By stripping your shelves and fridge down to the bare minimum you'll ensure a good turnover and freshness of food – and save an enormous amount of money. We also give a list of essential kitchen equipment, which will hopefully prevent the purchase of useless gadgets that remain unused in the back of a drawer. Then try our 'Storecupboard Suppers': spaghetti alla puttanesca (page 29) is a classic dish, and made using only ingredients from the cupboard – especially useful for when you have unexpected guests.

Cooking should be fun and simple, so we've made every effort to keep the number of ingredients and complicated techniques down to a minimum. Learn how to make entertaining family and friends an enjoyable experience. Try our 30-minute menu of pan-fried turkey wrapped in ham served with white bean mash, with coffee and chocolate trifles for dessert (pages 54–5) or, for something more exotic, sample our Moroccan feast (pages 40–3).

Eating a healthy diet has become increasingly important and we've made sure that every recipe featured in this book includes calorie and fat contents. For the even more health conscious, there's a chapter on low-fat cooking (page 58), which begins with low-fat dressings such as creamy blue cheese and thousand island (page 61), proving that you don't have to compromise on taste even if you are watching your weight. Even better, if you want a pudding without the guilt, try our low-fat apple crumble (page 76) or banana and chocolate chip muffins (page 84). The Basics chapter also has a useful list of low-fat storecupboard items (page 11).

For a working parent, feeding children is often a constant source of guilt and anxiety. In the inspired chapter, 'Busy Parents and Healthy Kids', we've taken classic children's recipes and adapted them so that they are both nutritious and easy to prepare. Vegetable gang lasagne (page 238) and baked potato fish pie (page 246) are guaranteed favourites.

So, whether you need inspiration for a new pasta dish, a fuss-free pudding or interesting vegetarian ideas, our collection of over 250 recipes will have the perfect solution for you.

the basics

Do you have a kitchen full of gadgets that have never been used or bottles of obscure ingredients sitting at the back of a cupboard? This chapter will help you organize, guiding you through essential equipment and products. Also included are comprehensive conversion tables and answers to some of the most commonly asked cookery questions.

essential equipment

Knives

A huge array of knives is not needed in the kitchen. You will mainly use a small preparation knife and a medium-sized cook's knife for chopping. A small serrated knife is very useful for slicing tomatoes and preparing fruit, but a good bread knife will work just as well. A knife sharpener, known as a steel, is as important as the knives; without regular sharpening even the best knives will become blunt.

The main feature you should look for in quality knives is a blade that runs through the handle of the knife – these knives are much safer to use. Buy knives with handles that feel comfortable, too. Although heavy knives are usually good quality, they can be difficult to manage.

Pots and pans

Look for good-quality pots and pans, usually reflected in the price tag. Stainless steel pans are practical and easy to clean, but check for sturdy handles. Plastic handles stay cooler to the touch but are likely to melt at some point. You will need a minimum of three saucepans: a large 20.5 cm (8 in) saucepan for pasta, a medium and a small one, all with lids, plus a good-sized casserole dish; cast-iron is best. A wok is useful – traditional steel ones need careful maintenance so try a non-stick version. Non-stick frying pans are the easiest to use but need hand-washing – one very large and one medium or small one are useful. A stove-top grill pan, especially a non-stick one, is a great extra. Make sure it is smoking hot when you cook on it.

Roasting tins and baking trays

Go for seriously good-quality products. Cheap tins buckle and won't lie flat on a surface, making burns and spills more likely. Make sure you choose sizes that fit easily in your oven, too. You will find a large and a small roasting tin and two or three baking trays good basic choices.

utensil checklist

American cup measures	Measuring jug
Baking trays	Measuring spoons
Can opener	Metal colander
Chopping board	Metal fish slice
Corkscrew	Metal pasta spoon
Electric whisk	Metal spoon
Frying pans	Mixing bowls
Garlic crusher	Ovenproof casserole
Grater	Pastry brush
Hand blender	Pepper mill
Ice cream scoop	Potato masher
Kitchen scales	Roasting tins
Kitchen scissors	Rubber spatula
Kitchen timer	Salad spinner
Kitchen tongs	Saucepans
Knives – small preparation	Sieve
knife, small serrated knife	Slotted metal spoon
(great for fruit), medium-	Vegetable swivel peeler
sized cook's knife and	Whisk
a bread knife	Wooden spoons
Ladle	Zester

conversion charts

American cup measures	USA	Metric	Imperial
Flour	1 cup	140 g	5 oz
Caster/granulated sugar	1 cup	225 g	8 oz
Brown sugar	1 cup	170 g	6 oz
Butter	1 cup	225 g	8 oz
Raisins	1 cup	200 g	7 oz
Ground almonds	1 cup	110 g	4 oz
Golden syrup	1 cup	340 g	12 oz
Uncooked rice	1 cup	200 g	7 oz
Grated cheese	1 cup	110 g	4 oz

Weights	
15 g	½ oz
25 g	1 oz
40 g	1½ oz
50 g	2 oz
75 g	3 oz
100 g	3½ oz
125 g	4 oz
150 g	5 oz
175 g	6 oz
200 g	7 oz
225 g	8 oz
250 g	9 oz
275 g	10 oz
300 g	11 oz
350 g	12 oz
375 g	13 oz
400 g	14 oz
425 g	15 oz
450 g	1 lb
500 g	1 lb 2 oz
550 g	1¼ lb
700 g	1½ lb
900 g	2 lb
1.1 kg	2½ lb
1.4 kg	3 lb
1.8 kg	4 lb
2 kg	4½ lb
2.3 kg	5 lb

Capacity	
25 ml	1 fl oz
50 ml	2 fl oz
150 ml	5 fl oz (¼ pint)
200 ml	7 fl oz (⅓ pint)
300 ml	10 fl oz (½ pint)
450 ml	15 fl oz (¾ pint)
600 ml	20 fl oz (1 pint)
750 ml	1¼ pints
900 ml	1½ pints
1 litre	1¾ pints
1.1 litres	2 pints
1.3 litres	2¼ pints
1.4 litres	2½ pints
1.6 litres	2¾ pints
1.7 litres	3 pints

Oven temperatures		
gas mark	°C	°F
¼	110	225
½	130	250
1	140	275
2	150	300
3	170	325
4	180	350
5	190	375
6	200	400
7	220	425
8	230	450
9	240	475

Teaspoons	
1.25 ml	¼ teaspoon
2.5 ml	½ teaspoon
3.75 ml	¾ teaspoon
5 ml	1 teaspoon
15 ml	1 tablespoon

It is recommended that you use size large eggs and level spoon measurements for all the recipes in this book, unless stated otherwise.

storecupboard ingredients

The fridge and freezer have been included along with storecupboard ingredients here as many essential ingredients keep well for weeks when chilled and for months when frozen. Also listed are special low-fat ingredients for the storecupboard. Choose whatever suits your particular cooking habits from the practical lists that follow.

In the cupboard:
Baking powder
Black peppercorns
Canned and bottled ingredients –
  anchovies in oil or salt, capers, sun-
  dried tomatoes, olives in oil, coconut
  milk, canned tomatoes, tuna, sweetcorn,
  chickpeas, butter beans, kidney beans,
  soup, fruit in fruit juice, passata, bottled
  pasta sauce and mango chutney
Cayenne pepper
Cooking alcohol – quarter bottles of wine,
  brandy, sherry and Madeira
Couscous
Custard powder
Dark chocolate (70 per cent cocoa solids)
Dried fruits and nuts – raisins, apricots,
  prunes, dates, pinenuts, cashews
  and almonds
Dried herbs and spices – oregano, mixed
  herbs, vanilla pods or vanilla extract,
  whole nutmeg, ground cinnamon,
  ground ginger, ground coriander
  and turmeric
Flour – white (look for unbleached),
  self-raising and plain
Lentils – Indian daal, green and puy
Oats
Oil – extra-virgin olive oil for salads, olive
oil for cooking and sunflower oil
Pasta – spaghetti, shapes such as
  penne or macaroni
Powdered milk
Rice – Arborio risotto rice, basmati rice
  and long-grain white rice

Salt
Sauces – soy sauce, Dijon mustard,
  English mustard powder, Worcestershire
  sauce, Tabasco, horseradish sauce, jam,
  tomato ketchup, mayonnaise and honey
Stock cubes – vegetable, chicken and beef
  (look for cubes or powders without
  monosodium glutamate)
Sugars – white caster, brown unrefined
  and demerara
Vinegar – white wine vinegar and
  balsamic vinegar

Low-fat storecupboard options:
Balsamic vinegar
Bulgar wheat
Canned beans and pulses
Canned tomatoes or passata
Chilli sauce
Consommé
Couscous
Dried mushrooms
Dried or puréed herbs and spices
English and French mustard
Hoisin, teriyaki and black bean sauce
Honey
Long-life fruit juices
Pasta and potato gnocchi
Polenta
Ready-to-eat dried fruit
Rice
Sweetcorn
Sweetened condensed skimmed milk
Sun-dried tomatoes
Tuna or salmon in brine

In the fridge:
The list below includes only those cooking ingredients with a fridge life of over a week. Always remember to bring eggs and milk to room temperature before using.

Bacon
Butter
Cheeses – Parmesan and cheddar
Chorizo sausage or salami
Crème fraîche
Eggs
Garlic
Long-life milk

In the freezer:
Below are just a few practical suggestions. The freezer can keep foods for up to six months; check the power rating of your freezer and the storage suggestions on the food to be frozen.

Frozen chips
Frozen herbs
Frozen vegetables – sweetcorn,
  peas and spinach
Ready-made frozen pastry – puff
  pastry and shortcrust pastry
Sliced bread

In freezer bags:
Fresh chillies, chopped
Fresh lemon grass, chopped
Fresh root ginger, peeled and grated

choosing ingredients and troubleshooting

The secret of successful cooking is choosing the right ingredients. Go for the best quality you can. The better the ingredients, the less elaborate the dish has to be. Good-quality dried pasta with a homemade tomato sauce is not only simple and fresh, but quick, nutritious and cheap.

Every one of us has an impact on the food production process. The more people who choose to support free-range, organic and carefully farmed produce, the more of this type of food we will see on our supermarket shelves.

Rice

There are many varieties of rice now easily available but pay attention to their different preparation techniques. Rice advertised as quick-cooking has been processed and partly cooked already.

Basmati – an Indian rice with a distinctive fragrance and long, thin grains. Always wash it before using.

Jasmine – also known as Thai fragrant rice, this rice is long grained but has a slightly sticky texture.

Risotto – varieties include Arborio and Carnaroli. This type of rice is able to absorb large amounts of liquid yet stay firm to the bite.

Sushi – a short-grained rice, sometimes described as glutenous rice, that become sticky when cooked.

Wild – the seeds of a type of water grass, rather than a rice. Wild rice is very expensive, has a nutty taste and chewy texture, and it is often sold ready-mixed with brown rice.

Brown – a whole rice which still retains the bran content. It takes longer to cook than white rice, but is very nutritious and full of flavour.

Problem: Watery, lumpy rice
Why? Overcooked; the rice has absorbed too much liquid and, as a result, has lost its shape and texture. Inferior long-grain white rice has a tendency to break down more easily because the grains are often damaged by processing.

Solution: Cook the rice in a large saucepan of boiling water and avoid low-quality rice.

Problem: Slightly crunchy, crispy rice
Why? Undercooked or burnt. This often happens in pilaf-style dishes if the rice is cooked over too high a heat, causing the bottom layer of rice to burn slightly if not enough liquid has been added or if some of the liquid has evaporated out of the pan during the cooking process.

Solution: Follow the recipe very carefully; pilafs can also be cooked in the oven if you are worried about maintaining a low temperature. As a general rule rice absorbs about twice its volume in liquid, so add two measures of liquid per measure of rice.

Pasta

Authentic Italian-style pasta is made from durum wheat flour – look for this in the ingredients for a good texture. Durum wheat pasta retains a slight bite when cooked correctly. Endless varieties of pasta are available in different shapes and ingredients. See below for which shapes of pasta to use with which type of sauce.

Problem: Claggy, sticky pasta
Why? The water was not boiling properly. The pasta needs to move freely in the water to stop it sticking.

Solution: Keep an eye on the saucepan and make sure the water boils over a high heat.

Problem: Baked pasta dish very crunchy
Why? Not enough sauce; the pasta has dried out.

Solution: Pasta needs to be thoroughly covered with a sauce when baked, not just coated in it. If you like a crispy topping, top baked pasta dishes with a thick layer of breadcrumbs mixed with cheese and place under a grill until golden.

Noodles

Only specialized oriental food shops sell fresh oriental noodles. The most commonly available ones in supermarkets are the dried versions, including Chinese egg noodles, rice noodles, vermicelli and Japanese soba noodles.

Noodles for stir-frying:
Chinese egg noodles – these are readily available dried but must be cooked before adding to stir-fries. They can also be added to soups.

Rice noodles – these flat, wide noodles are great for Thai dishes. Soak them in cool water before using.

Noodles for soups and salads:
Rice vermicelli – round, fine noodles used for cold salads and hot in soups. Soak before use.

Soba noodles – these Japanese buckwheat flour noodles have a distinctive nutty flavour. They must be boiled but you will need to follow the cooking instructions on the packet carefully .

Problem: All the noodles have stuck to the frying pan or wok in a stir-fry recipe
Why? The noodles were not properly drained after boiling or not rinsed after cooking to remove excess starch. The frying pan was not hot enough when the noodles were added.

Solution: Always rinse noodles in cold running water after boiling and drain well. Ensure the stir-fry pan is really hot and, if frying the noodles on their own, that a small amount of hot oil is in the pan first.

Pasta shapes – shapes are ideal for pasta bakes, hearty soups and cold salads, as well as for serving with chunky sauces; the rougher the sauce texture, the larger the pasta shapes you should use. Examples include penne, farfalle, conchiglie, rigatoni, gnochetti and ziti.

Long pasta – these shapes of pasta suit sauces that will cling to the strands, such as creamy cheese sauces and thick tomato sauces. Examples of the widest long pasta are pappardelle, tagliatelle and lasagne sheets; of medium width are spaghetti, fettuccine and bucatini; while tagliolini, linguine, spaghettini and capellini are among the thinnest varieties of long pasta.

Fresh or dried? Very good-quality fresh pasta is available from Italian delicatessens; the packaged variety sold elsewhere is of inferior quality and designed to be quick-cooking and have an extensive fridge life – it is not really 'fresh' at all. Good-quality Italian dried pasta is recommended for all the pasta recipes in this book.

Problem: The noodles have stuck together in lumps in a stir-fry recipe
Why? If the noodles are not cooled with cold water after boiling, they will continue to cook while standing and stick together.

Solution: Ensure noodles are cooled with cold running water, then tip them into a bowl and add a few drops of an oil (sesame is best) to ensure that they do not stick together.

Meat
The two qualities that everyone wants in meat are good flavour and tenderness. The cuts that are quickest to cook, the leanest and the most tender, such as fillet steak, pork tenderloin and lamb steaks, will have the least amount of flavour. The good news is that the cheaper cuts of meat are usually packed with flavour! These cuts need long cooking, but the result is very tender, tasty meat.

Q: I want to make roast pork with crackling. Which cut of pork should I use?

A: Use loin of pork with skin. Score through the fat before cooking and sprinkle it with salt to ensure a crisp crackling.

Q: Which is the best cut to use for a Moroccan-style braised lamb dish?

A: A braise is just another word for a stew. Many cuts can be used, such as scrag end and leg of lamb, but the easiest is boned shoulder. Cut it into large cubes and remove big pieces of fat. Don't worry about trimming the meat too carefully as some fat melts during cooking, helping to make the meat more tender.

Q: I love rare steak but never seem to cook it correctly – by the time I serve it, it is always at least medium. Help!

A: It is important to choose a steak that is about 2 cm (¾ in) thick in order to be able to get it hot, yet rare at the same time. For example, thin frying steaks cook in no time and are almost impossible to serve below medium. Use sirloin or fillet steak.
For extra tenderness, after frying, allow the meat to rest in a warm place, such as a low oven, for 5 minutes before serving. For a 2 cm (¾ in) thick steak at cool room temperature, cooked in a very hot pan, use the following timings:
   rare: 1½ minutes per side
   medium rare: 2 minutes per side
   medium: 2½ minutes per side
   well done: 3–4 minutes per side

Q: When I buy freshly minced beef at a butcher's, it goes slightly brown on the surface after a day in the fridge. Is it still safe to use? Supermarket mince doesn't seem to do this.

A: All that has happened is the surface of the meat has come into contact with air and oxidized slightly. If it is tightly wrapped it should not brown. It is safe to cook unless a very strong, bad odour comes off the meat. Supermarket beef rarely changes colour as it is packaged under conditions to prevent this.

Poultry
Although chicken is by far the most popular option, turkey and duck are both readily available and make an interesting change.

Chicken – battery-reared chicken is by far the cheapest, but it is flavourless and has a watery texture. Try corn-fed chicken, which has slightly yellow skin, or a good free-range bird. Poussin is simply a young chicken that is not fully grown.

Turkey – its breast is slightly stronger flavoured than chicken and the texture a little tougher, but it can be delicious in stir-fries and curries.

Duck – breasts are often regarded as fatty, but the meat is quite lean. Trim off as much fat as you wish from the breast, although some helps keep the meat moist. Duck legs are meltingly tender when braised.

Q: When I make chicken curry, I often find the chicken becomes very tough.

A: The chicken is probably overcooked, which is easy to do, especially with breast meat. Boneless chicken thighs are ideal in curries as they take longer to cook and so have time to absorb the curry flavours. When you add breast meat to the sauce, simmer very gently and do not boil. Chicken breast cooks very quickly, so try testing a piece after 3–4 minutes – the meat should be white in the centre. For added flavour, marinate breasts in spices overnight first.

Q: I would like to try cooking duck breasts. It is all right to serve them pink?

A: Yes. Unlike chicken, duck can be cooked from medium rare to well done.

Fish and Seafood

Many people still lack confidence when it comes to choosing and cooking fish and seafood. Fish is cooked at a much lower temperature than other meats, but becomes dry and very tasteless when overcooked. Ideally, shellfish should be bought alive. Crabs and lobsters should feel heavy in relation to size, and the shells of mussels or clams should be tightly shut and undamaged before cooking. Follow cooking timings precisely as seafood can easily become overcooked, tasting rubbery and chewy.

Poaching – the fish is covered or partly covered in a liquid, such as stock or white wine, and then gently heated until the liquid just starts to simmer. Never let the poaching liquid boil, or the fish will toughen.

Steaming – the fish is placed in a tightly fitting perforated container over a pan of boiling water or stock. The steam produced by the boiling liquid cooks the fish. This is a healthy way to cook fish as it retains all its nutrients and natural flavour.

Grilling – this method is suitable for oily fish, such as herring, mackerel and sardines. If the fish is thin or only a fillet, the flesh or cut side should be cooked first to seal in juices. Always preheat the grill to its highest setting so the fish seals quickly.

Baking – this is a good way to cook large fish joints. Simply cover the fish in a little stock and butter or oil. You can also bake fish in pastry or foil.

Shallow-frying – use a combination of butter and oil; the butter gives flavour while the oil prevents the butter from burning. If you have a non-stick pan, you can cook the fish with no added fat, which is a much healthier way of frying fish.

Roasting – this is good for cooking whole fish, cuts of firm fish and lobster. To roast fish, you need an oven temperature of gas mark 6–8/200–230°C (400–450°F). If the oven is not hot enough and the roasting tin is not preheated, the juices from the fish will escape and the fish will boil rather than roast.

red onion and prune relish
MAKES 1.8 KG (4 LB) • PREP 20 MINS •
COOK 1 HR 35 MINS • CALS PER TBSP (15 ML) 27 •
FAT PER TBSP (15 ML) 1 G

125 ml (4 fl oz) olive oil
1.5 kg (3¼ lb) red onions, sliced
225 g (8 oz) ready-to-eat prunes, chopped
200 ml (7 fl oz) red wine
375 g (13 oz) demerara sugar
200 ml (7 fl oz) red wine vinegar
1 teaspoon pink peppercorns
1 teaspoon juniper berries

1 Heat some olive oil in a large frying pan or wok. Add the onions, a little at a time, adding more olive oil as you need it. Stir all the time, until the onions begin to soften and turn a wonderful pink colour, then simmer gently for 30 minutes.
2 Add the prunes and stir in the wine. Cook for 10 minutes. Then add the sugar and vinegar and simmer until the mixture begins to thicken.
3 Remove from the heat and season with salt and ground black pepper. Add the peppercorns and juniper berries. Leave the relish to cool completely, then spoon it into sterilized jars, seal and store (see page 16).

piccalilli

MAKES 1.1 KG (2½ LB) • PREP 15 MINS • COOK 25 MINS •
CALS PER TBSP (15 ML) 8 • FAT PER TBSP (15 ML) 0 G

225 g (8 oz) cauliflower floret, broken into
 small pieces
1 onion, finely chopped
900 ml (1½ pints) white wine vinegar
2 teaspoons mustard seeds
1 teaspoon pink peppercorns
4 tablespoons demerara sugar
175 g (6 oz) courgette, diced
175 g (6 oz) cucumber, diced
175 g (6 oz) marrow, diced
1 tablespoon ground turmeric
1 tablespoon ground ginger
1 tablespoon mustard powder
3 tablespoons cornflour

1 Cook the cauliflower and onion in half the
vinegar for 5 minutes. Add salt and black
pepper, mustard seeds, peppercorns and sugar.
Stir well, then add the remaining vegetables.
2 Make a thin paste with the turmeric, ginger,
mustard powder and remaining vinegar, and
add to the vegetables. Stir well and cook
gently for 5 minutes.
3 Blend the cornflour in a cup with a little water
and add to the pan. Bring to the boil, stirring
constantly as it starts to thicken, then simmer
gently for 10 minutes.
4 Pour into sterilized jars, seal and store (see
below). Serve with cold meats and cheese.

Sterilizing and Sealing Jars
To sterilize jars, wash them first and then stand
them upside down on a wire rack on a baking
sheet. Place in the oven at gas mark 4/180°C
(350°F) for 20 minutes. Allow to cool slightly
before filling, but don't let the jars get too cold
or they will crack when you add hot vinegar.
Fill to the top and cover, while still hot, with
a wax disc and then with dampened cellophane,
securing with a rubber band. For longterm
storage, cover with a lid when cold.

roasted tomato chutney

MAKES 1.4 KG (3 LB) • PREP 20 MINS • COOK 2 HRS •
CALS PER TBSP (15 ML) 13 • FAT PER TBSP (15 ML) 0 G

6 tomatoes, left whole,
 plus 1.4 kg (3 lb) tomatoes, skinned
 and chopped
1 tablespoon olive oil
2 onions, finely chopped
175 g (6 oz) demerara sugar
600 ml (1 pint) cider vinegar
2 teaspoons ground allspice
2 teaspoons ground cloves
2 teaspoons ground cinnamon
2 teaspoons mustard seeds
1 teaspoon dill seeds

1 Preheat the oven to gas mark 8/230°C (450°F). Place the whole tomatoes in a roasting tin and, using your hands, coat them with the olive oil so that they are well covered. Roast them in the oven for 20–30 minutes, until they are beginning to char, then set aside.

2 Place the skinned tomatoes, chopped onions, sugar and vinegar in a large saucepan and bring to the boil. Reduce to a simmer and add the ground spices, mustard and dill seeds. Continue to simmer for 30 minutes, until the mixture is greatly reduced. When the chutney is cooked and reduced enough, the mixture should be so thick that when a space is made in it with a wooden spoon, it doesn't fill up with vinegar.

3 Roughly chop the charred tomatoes and add to the tomato and onion mixture. Season with salt and ground black pepper and allow to cool. When cool, spoon the chutney into sterilized jars, seal and store (see page 16).

vegetable stock

Some vegetables are too strongly flavoured or will make a cloudy stock. For a basic, balanced flavour, start with **carrots, onions, celery** and a **bay leaf**. You can also include **shallots, garlic, tomatoes, mushrooms, leeks, fennel, parsley, peas** (and pea pods), **thyme** and **basil stalks**. Do not include potatoes, cabbage, asparagus, beetroot, sweet potato, cucumber or rosemary.

Making tasty, nutritious vegetable stock is as easy as throwing your chosen vegetables, washed and roughly chopped, into a large saucepan, covering them with cold water and simmering for about 1 hour. You can also add **white wine** or **vermouth**. Then strain the stock, leave to cool and refrigerate or freeze.

oriental vegetable soup

This is about as healthy as possible – and so good! Heat 250 ml (8 fl oz) **vegetable stock** per person. Add a little sliced **fresh root ginger**, a handful of **chopped spinach** or Chinese cabbage per person, **beansprouts, sliced peppers, carrots, mushrooms** and any other vegetables you like. Sliced **tofu** is also delicious, as are **egg noodles**. Simmer for 2 minutes, season with **soy sauce** and serve in large soup bowls.

vinaigrette

MAKES 140 ML (5 FL OZ) • PREP 5 MINS • COOK NONE • CALS PER TBSP (15 ML) 70 • FAT PER TBSP (15 ML) 7 G

1 tablespoon Dijon mustard
2 tablespoons red wine or balsamic vinegar
1 teaspoon honey
6 tablespoons olive oil

1 In a bowl whisk together the mustard, vinegar, a pinch of salt and freshly ground pepper.
2 Stir in the honey then slowly whisk in the oil until well combined. Check the taste, adding more oil if necessary.

mayonnaise

MAKES 300 ML (10 FL OZ) • PREP 15 MINS • COOK NONE •
CALS PER TBSP (15 ML) 104 • FAT PER TBSP (15 ML) 11 G

2 egg yolks
1 teaspoon white wine vinegar or lemon juice
1 teaspoon English mustard powder
300 ml (½ pint) light oil, such as grapeseed
   or sunflower

1 In a large bowl, mix together the egg yolks,
vinegar or lemon juice and mustard powder,
then add 2 tablespoons water.
2 Slowly add the oil, drop by drop to start with,
until incorporated. An electric hand-whisk makes
this easier. Season, adding more vinegar or a
little water if too thick.

herb pistou

This is a great dressing for pasta, fish, salads
and chicken, and pistou is a good way to keep
fresh herbs. Once made into a paste, the herb
pistou will keep for a few weeks in the fridge,
covered in olive oil in a sealed container.

You can use **parsley**, **basil**, **coriander** or a
mixture – just place a good handful in a food
processor, add about ½ fresh **garlic clove** and
pulse to chop. Slowly pour in enough **olive oil**
to make a paste, thinning it to your liking. Add
salt, **pepper** and a squeeze of **lemon juice**. To
make the more substantial pesto, add grated
Parmesan and toasted pinenuts or almonds.

fresh tomato sauce

SERVES 4 • PREP 10 MINS • COOK 25 MINS •
CALS PER PORTION 150 • FAT PER PORTION 9 G

10 large, ripe tomatoes, halved
1 small red onion, peeled and very
   roughly chopped
1 garlic clove, peeled and halved
3 tablespoons olive oil
1 teaspoon dried oregano
   or mixed herbs

1 Preheat the oven to gas mark 6/200°C (400°F).
2 Place all the ingredients in a large roasting
tin, season generously with salt and freshly
ground black pepper, stir well and roast for
about 25 minutes.
3 When cooked, tip the ingredients into a bowl
or food processor and blend until smooth. Thin
with a little water if necessary.

Variation

To turn the fresh tomato sauce into a delicious
soup, simply add 250 ml (8 fl oz) vegetable or
chicken stock to the sauce and heat gently to
serve. If desired, top the soup with Parmesan
and a swirl of olive oil.

winter tomato sauce

SERVES 4 • PREP 5 MINS • COOK 30 MINS •
CALS PER PORTION 100 • FAT PER PORTION 6 G

2 tablespoons olive oil
1 large onion, finely chopped
4 button mushrooms, finely chopped
   (optional)
1 teaspoon sugar
1 garlic clove, crushed
2 x 400 g (14 oz) cans chopped tomatoes

1 In a saucepan, heat the olive oil. Add the
onions, mushrooms, if using, and sugar. Cook
over a gentle heat for about 10 minutes until
the vegetables are soft.
2 Add the garlic, cook for 1 minute and then add
the canned tomatoes. Season well with salt and
black pepper, and simmer for 20 minutes.

shortcrust pastry

MAKES 225 G (8 OZ) • PREP 10 MINS PLUS RESTING •
COOK NONE • TOTAL CALS 1581 • TOTAL FAT 93 G

225 g (8 oz) flour
50 g (2 oz) butter, cubed
50 g (2 oz) lard, cubed
3–4 tablespoons cold water

1 In a large bowl, sift flour, add a pinch of salt
and add the butter and lard. Using fingertips,
rub butter and lard into the flour until the
mixture looks like fine breadcrumbs.
2 Gradually add the egg yolks and just enough
very cold water (about 50 ml/2 fl oz) to bind
the mixture to a dough – be careful not to add
too much. Wrap and chill the pastry for at least
1 hour before use.

Tip
Shortcrust, one of the most versatile pastries
for tarts and flans, is easy to make and freezes
brilliantly. Seal it in an airtight plastic bag and
store in the freezer for up to a month.

lemon and thyme curd

MAKES 400 ML (14 FL OZ) • PREP 10 MINS •
COOK 40 MINS • CALS PER TBSP (15 ML) 55 •
FAT PER TBSP (15 ML) 3G

175 g (6 oz) caster sugar
2 medium eggs, lightly beaten
2 medium egg yolks
2 sprigs of fresh thyme
75 g (3 oz) butter, cut into small cubes
grated zest and juice of 2 lemons

1 Put the sugar, eggs, egg yolks, sprigs of
thyme, butter and lemon zest and juice in
a heatproof bowl set over a saucepan of
barely simmering water.
2 Gently heat until the butter has melted and
the sugar has dissolved, stirring occasionally.
3 Increase the heat so the water is simmering,
and continue to heat the mixture for 30 minutes,
stirring occasionally until it thickens.
4 Remove the bowl from the heat and allow the
lemon curd to cool.
5 Remove the thyme, then pour the curd into
sterilized jars and seal (see page 16). Store in
the fridge for up to a month. It is ideal on toast,
or heated gently and served as a sauce.

storecupboard suppers

Most people think stocking a storecupboard merely means filling it with assorted jars and cans. Try to widen this perception by also using your fridge and freezer as highly effective storecupboards (see page 11). With a bit of careful planning, making quick, nutritious meals will become an easier task – even when the shops are closed.

green lentil and cranberry salad

SERVES 8–10 • PREP 25 MINS • COOK NONE • CALS PER PORTION 170 • FAT PER PORTION 5 G

1 In a bowl, soak the cranberries in the orange juice until they become nice and plump.

2 In a large bowl, mix together the orange zest, green lentils and parsley, then stir in the soaked cranberries and juice.

3 In a bowl, whisk together the olive oil and white wine vinegar, then pour over the lentil mixture. Toss together and season well with salt and ground black pepper. Serve with cold meats.

2 x 75 g (3 oz) packets dried cranberries

grated zest and juice of 2 small oranges

3 x 450 g (1 lb) cans green lentils, drained and rinsed

2 x 20 g (¾ oz) packets fresh flat leaf parsley

4 tablespoons olive oil

1 tablespoon white wine vinegar

pepper, chorizo and chickpea salad

SERVES 4 • PREP 15 MINS • COOK 10 MINS • CALS PER PORTION 480 • FAT PER PORTION 28 G

150 g (5 oz) chorizo sausage, thinly sliced

1 teaspoon cumin seeds

4 Romero peppers

2 x 410 g (approx 14 oz) cans chickpeas, drained

5 tablespoons olive oil

2 tablespoons sherry vinegar

1 bird's eye chilli, finely sliced

4 tablespoons fresh parsley, finely chopped

1 In a large frying pan, fry the chorizo until crispy. Drain on kitchen paper and set aside. Add the cumin seeds to the frying pan and fry for 20 seconds, remove and set aside. Place the peppers on an oiled baking tray and cook under a preheated grill for 5 minutes, until cooked and the skins are slightly charred.
2 In a large bowl, combine the chickpeas, olive oil, sherry vinegar, cumin seeds, chilli and parsley. Season well with salt and ground black pepper. To serve, place a pepper on each plate, top with the chickpea mixture and scatter over the chorizo.

Tips
Chorizo is a spicy Spanish sausage available in supermarkets. Romero peppers are long peppers that look like large chillies – if you can't find them, use 4 regular peppers instead.

fruity couscous salad

SERVES 8 • PREP 15 MINS • COOK NONE • CALS PER PORTION 250 • FAT PER PORTION 12 G

1 Put the couscous in a bowl and cover with 350 ml (12 fl oz) boiling water and 1 tablespoon olive oil. Leave to stand for 10 minutes until water is absorbed. Fluff up with a fork, then set aside to cool.

2 Fold the chopped apricots, walnut halves and coriander into the couscous. Pour in the lemon juice and remaining olive oil, season with salt and ground black pepper, stir until well combined and then serve.

2 x 175 g (6 oz) packets couscous

3 tablespoons olive oil

225 g (8 oz) dried apricots, roughly chopped

100 g (3½ oz) packet walnut halves

1 small bunch of fresh coriander, chopped

juice of 1 lemon

pumpkin risotto

SERVES 4 • PREP 20 MINS • COOK 30 MINS • CALS PER PORTION 645 • FAT PER PORTION 24 G

2 tablespoons olive oil

1 small onion, finely chopped

375 g (13 oz) Arborio rice

175 ml (6 fl oz) white wine

700 g (1½ lb) pumpkin, the flesh scooped out and chopped into small chunks, seeds discarded

1 sprig of fresh rosemary

1 vegetable stock cube, made up with 1.1–1.4 litres (2–2½ pints) boiling water

75 g (3 oz) butter

50 g (2 oz) Parmesan, grated

1 In a large pan, heat the oil. Add the onion and cook for about 5–6 minutes until soft. Stir in the rice and cook, stirring for 1–2 minutes. Add the wine and simmer for a few minutes until there is about a tablespoon of wine left.

2 Add the pumpkin flesh and sprig of rosemary and add a ladleful of hot stock to the rice, stirring well. Bring to the boil then reduce the heat to a simmer. As the liquid is absorbed, gradually add more stock, a ladleful at a time, stirring frequently until the rice is cooked – about 20 minutes. To serve, stir in the butter and Parmesan and season with salt and black pepper.

Variations

If you cannot get hold of pumpkin, use butternut squash instead. Alternatively, make up the stock with a good fresh pumpkin soup mixed with vegetable stock.

tuscan soup

SERVES 4 • PREP 5 MINS • COOK 25 MINS • CALS PER PORTION 200 • FAT PER PORTION 7 G

1 In a heavy-based saucepan, heat 1 tablespoon of the oil and gently fry the onion and garlic for 3–4 minutes until soft. Add the pancetta or bacon and continue to fry for 5 minutes until crispy. Add the beans, frozen herbs, stock and red wine. Bring to the boil and simmer for 5 minutes.

2 Add the passata, bring the soup back to the boil and simmer for 10 minutes. Season with salt and ground black pepper, and serve in soup bowls with a drizzle of the remaining oil.

Tip

Passata is smooth, thick-sieved or creamed tomatoes. You'll find it packaged in cartons or jars in large supermarkets. Cartons of passata can be frozen.

2 tablespoons olive oil

1 onion, finely chopped

2 garlic cloves, crushed

125 g (4 oz) pancetta or bacon pieces, defrosted

400 g (14 oz) can butter beans, drained and rinsed

2 tablespoons frozen mixed herbs

150 ml (¼ pint) vegetable stock

150 ml (¼ pint) red wine

500 g (1 lb 2 oz) carton passata

gnocchi with fresh tomato sauce

SERVES 4 • PREP 45 MINS • COOK 50 MINS • CALS PER PORTION 606 • FAT PER PORTION 23 G

12 plum tomatoes, halved

4 garlic cloves, crushed

grated zest of ½ lemon

1 large bunch of fresh basil, roughly torn

3 tablespoons olive oil

500 g (1 lb 2 oz) packet gnocchi

2 tablespoons tomato purée

150 g (5 oz) packet mozzarella, drained and sliced

25 g (1 oz) Parmesan, grated

1 Preheat the oven to gas mark 6/200°C (400°F). Place the tomatoes, cut side up, in a large roasting tin. Sprinkle the garlic, lemon zest, half the basil and the oil over the tomatoes. Roast for 30–35 minutes or until lightly charred.
2 Cook the gnocchi in a saucepan of boiling water, according to packet instructions. When cooked, remove with a slotted spoon and keep warm.
3 Mash the tomatoes to make a rough sauce. Add the tomato purée, the remaining basil and season with salt and pepper.
4 Add the drained gnocchi to the tomato sauce and transfer to a heatproof dish. Top with the mozzarella slices and sprinkle with the Parmesan. Cook for 15–20 minutes until piping hot and the cheese has melted.

Tips
Gnocchi are small dumplings made out of flour, semolina, potato or choux pastry. The word literally means lump. They are available ready-made dried or fresh. For a good shortcut make up double quantities of the tomato sauce and freeze. This sauce can also be served with pasta or grilled chicken.

creamy spaghetti

SERVES 4 • PREP 5 MINS • COOK 15 MINS • CALS PER PORTION 790 • FAT PER PORTION 46 G

1 Cook the spaghetti in a pan of boiling, salted water according to packet instructions. Meanwhile, in a saucepan melt the butter and fry the garlic for 1 minute.

2 Add the double cream and peas to the garlic. Bring gently to the boil and simmer for 5 minutes, stirring to combine until the sauce thickens slightly and the peas are tender. Then stir in half of the grated Parmesan and season with salt and black pepper.

3 Drain the spaghetti. Pour over the sauce and add the mint, stirring thoroughly to coat. Sprinkle the remaining Parmesan on top to serve.

375 g (13 oz) dried spaghetti

25 g (1 oz) butter

1 garlic clove, crushed

284 ml (approx ½ pint) carton double cream

225 g (8 oz) frozen peas

50 g (2 oz) Parmesan, grated

2 tablespoons fresh or frozen mint, roughly chopped

spaghetti alla puttanesca

SERVES 4 • PREP 10 MINS • COOK 25 MINS • CALS PER PORTION 590 • FAT PER PORTION 14 G

2 tablespoons olive oil

4 garlic cloves, crushed

2 small red chillies, deseeded and finely chopped

2 x 50 g (2 oz) cans anchovies, roughly chopped

3 tablespoons capers

100 g (3½ oz) pitted black olives, halved

2 x 400 g (14 oz) cans plum tomatoes

500 g (1 lb 2 oz) packet dried spaghetti

1 bunch of fresh basil, roughly torn

1 In a large saucepan, heat the oil over a moderate heat. Add the garlic and chillies and cook for 1 minute until the garlic is just golden. Add the anchovies, capers, olives and canned tomatoes with their juice and bring to the boil. Reduce the heat and simmer for 20–25 minutes until the sauce is thick.

2 Meanwhile, cook the spaghetti in a saucepan of boiling, salted water according to packet instructions. To serve, drain the cooked pasta and toss with the tomato sauce. Add the basil and season with salt and ground black pepper.

neopolitan pizza

SERVES 2 • PREP 10 MINS • COOK 15 MINS • CALS PER PORTION 500 • FAT PER PORTION 26 G

1 Preheat the oven to gas mark 6/200°C (400°F). Place the pizza base on a baking tray. Spread the base with the pizza topping, then sprinkle over the chilli flakes, lemon zest and garlic.
2 Scatter the anchovies, olives and mozzarella on top. Season generously with salt and ground black pepper. Bake in the oven for 10–15 minutes until the base is crispy and golden.

20.5 cm (8 in) pizza base

4 tablespoons ready-made pizza topping

1 teaspoon crushed chilli flakes

grated zest of ½ lemon

1 garlic clove, crushed

50 g (2 oz) can anchovy fillets in oil, drained

50 g (2 oz) pitted, mixed olives

125 g (4 oz) mini mozzarella balls

gruyère, artichoke and olive tart

SERVES 6 • PREP 35 MINS • COOK 35–40 MINS • CALS PER PORTION 360 • FAT PER PORTION 25 G

1 Preheat the oven to gas mark 4/180°C (350°F). Lightly grease a 25.5 cm (10 in) loose-bottomed tin or a 35.5 x 11.5 cm (14 x 4½ in) oblong tin.

2 Roll out the pastry and use it to line the greased tin, tucking it well up the sides, then chill for 20 minutes. Place greaseproof paper on top of the pastry with its edges overlapping and fill with baking beans, or dried peas, to weigh it down. Bake in the oven for 15 minutes until lightly golden. Remove the baking beans and greaseproof paper and leave the pastry case to cool.

3 In a small saucepan, heat the olive oil. Add the spring onions and cook gently to soften. Spread them over the base of the cooked pastry case, sprinkle with the Gruyère cheese, then arrange the artichokes and olives on top.

4 Whisk together the eggs, milk and mustard, season with salt and black pepper, and then pour over the tart. Return to the oven for a further 15–20 minutes until lightly set and golden. Allow to cool, then slice and serve with the green salad leaves.

340 g (approx 12 oz) packet shortcrust pastry

1 tablespoon olive oil

1 bunch of spring onions, sliced

150 g (5 oz) Gruyère cheese, grated

425 g (15 oz) can artichokes, drained and halved

12 green olives

2 eggs

200 ml (7 fl oz) milk

1 teaspoon Dijon mustard

green salad leaves, such as rocket

tortilla wraps

SERVES 4 • PREP 10 MINS • COOK NONE • CALS PER PORTION 350 • FAT PER PORTION 8 G

2 x 390 g (approx 14 oz) cans ratatouille

1 teaspoon fennel seeds

4 tortilla wraps

100 g (3½ oz) goats' cheese, cubed

1 In a bowl mix together the ratatouille and fennel seeds.
2 Spoon the mixture onto the tortilla wraps and scatter over the goats' cheese. Season well with salt and ground black pepper and roll up the wraps. Cut them in half diagonally and serve cold.

chicken jambalaya

SERVES 4 • PREP 5 MINS • COOK 25 MINS • CALS PER PORTION 860 • FAT PER PORTION 51 G

2 tablespoons olive oil

2 large frozen chicken breasts, defrosted, cut into small cubes

2 x 110 g (approx 3½ oz) packets chorizo sausage, finely sliced

250 g (9 oz) long-grain rice

2 'Mexican-flavoured' stock cubes

125 g (4 oz) cashew nuts

3 celery sticks, finely sliced

2 tablespoons fresh coriander, roughly chopped

1 In a large, heavy-based saucepan, heat the oil and fry the chicken for 5 minutes until sealed and brown. Transfer to a plate. Fry the chorizo for a few minutes, until crispy and beginning to curl. Set aside with the chicken and drain the fat from the pan.
2 Return the chicken and chorizo to the pan, add the rice and sprinkle over the Mexican stock cubes. Pour in 1 litre (1¾ pints) boiling water, bring to the boil and simmer for 10 minutes, stirring occasionally.
3 Meanwhile, in a frying pan dry-fry the cashews for 2–4 minutes until toasted. Add the celery to the rice mixture and simmer for a further 10 minutes until all the water is absorbed. Remove from the heat and season generously. Add the cashews and chopped coriander and serve.

Variation
If you can't find 'Mexican-flavoured' stock cubes, replace the quantity with 1 teaspoon chilli powder, 1 teaspoon ground cumin and 1 teaspoon paprika.

veggie curry

SERVES 4 • PREP 5 MINS • COOK 25 MINS • CALS PER PORTION 380 • FAT PER PORTION 12 G

1 tablespoon olive oil

1 onion, cut into thin wedges

4–6 tablespoons balti curry paste (depending on hotness)

150 g (5 oz) red lentils, rinsed

225 g (8 oz) frozen or fresh spinach

230 g (approx 8 oz) can chopped tomatoes

240 g (approx 8½ oz) can chickpeas, drained

naan bread, to serve (optional)

1 In a heavy-based saucepan, heat the oil and fry the onion for 5 minutes until soft. Add the curry paste, lentils and 750 ml (1¼ pints) boiling water. Stir to dissolve the paste, bring to the boil and then simmer for 10 minutes.

2 Add the spinach in batches, stirring until wilted. Add the tomatoes and chickpeas, mix thoroughly, cover and simmer for 10 minutes. Season with salt and ground black pepper, then serve, with warmed naan bread if desired.

Variation

If you don't like hot curry, replace the balti paste with another version, such as korma for a milder taste.

salmon laksa

SERVES 4 • PREP 5 MINS • COOK 10 MINS • CALS PER PORTION 360 • FAT PER PORTION 20 G

1 Pour the coconut milk, fish stock and Thai curry paste into a large, heavy-based saucepan and bring to the boil.
2 Add the salmon and noodles, bring back to the boil and simmer for 5 minutes. Add the spring onions, season with salt and ground black pepper and simmer for a final 5 minutes. Serve in soup bowls and garnish with fresh coriander.

400 ml (14 fl oz) can reduced-fat coconut milk

600 ml (1 pint) fresh fish stock

3 teaspoons red Thai curry paste

300 g (11 oz) skinless, boneless salmon fillet

125 g (4 oz) thick egg noodles

8 spring onions, finely sliced

2 tablespoons fresh coriander, roughly chopped

pork and fennel bake

SERVES 4 • PREP 5 MINS • COOK 25 MINS • CALS PER PORTION 600 • FAT PER PORTION 32 G

1 Preheat the oven to gas mark 6/200°C (400°F). Grease a shallow pie dish and arrange the fennel and raw pork cubes in the bottom. Parboil the potatoes for 5 minutes in a saucepan of boiling, salted water. Run the potatoes under cool water until cold, then peel.

2 In a bowl, mix the white wine sauce and cream, then pour it over the pork and fennel. Grate the parboiled potatoes on top of the mixture, making sure that it is completely covered. Season with salt and ground black pepper and drizzle with the oil.

3 Bake in the oven for 20 minutes until crisp and golden, and serve with fresh seasonal vegetables.

1 fennel bulb, sliced lengthways

500 g (1 lb 2 oz) frozen pork, defrosted, cubed

3 large potatoes, halved

435 g (approx 15½ oz) jar white wine sauce

4 tablespoons double cream

1 tablespoon olive oil

smoked gammon
with white bean and cabbage mash

SERVES 4 • PREP 10 MINS • COOK 15 MINS • CALS PER PORTION 690 • FAT PER PORTION 33 G

1 Preheat an oven grill. In a large bowl, mix together the mustard, vinegar and honey. Add the gammon steaks and stir well to coat. Cook under the grill for 3–5 minutes each side until golden brown and cooked through.

2 Meanwhile, make the bean and cabbage mash. Melt the butter in a large saucepan, add the butter beans and mash until a purée is formed. Heat the semi-skimmed milk and stir it into the bean mash with lots of ground black pepper.

3 Either put the cabbage in a large bowl with 2 tablespoons water, cover with clear film and microwave on HIGH for 2 minutes or add to a saucepan of boiling water and cook for 1 minute. Drain and stir into the bean mixture.

4 Serve the gammon steaks with the bean and cabbage mash, plenty of mustard and a good fruit chutney.

Tip

Smoked gammon steaks can be a little salty, so be wary of adding any more salt.

2 teaspoons Dijon mustard

1 tablespoon sherry or cider vinegar

2 tablespoons runny honey

4 smoked gammon steaks

75 g (3 oz) butter

3 x 410 g (approx 14 oz) cans butter beans, drained and rinsed

125 ml (4 fl oz) semi-skimmed milk

200 g (7 oz) Savoy cabbage, thinly sliced

3

easy entertaining

A few basic tips will take all the stress out of entertaining: never attempt a new complicated recipe when you've got guests coming over; keep it simple; and use quality ingredients. Pasta and a green salad, dressed with olive oil and fresh Parmesan, is easy to make and people will love it.

moroccan salad with pistachio dressing

SERVES 6 • PREP 10 MINS • COOK NONE • CALS PER PORTION 130 • FAT PER PORTION 12 G

1 Make the dressing by whisking together the lemon juice, olive oil and ground cinnamon. Season with salt and black pepper.
2 Just before serving, toss the grated carrot, rocket, sliced red onion and chopped mint and pistachios with the dressing in a large bowl and serve immediately.

Tip
This salad can be served either as a starter or as an accompaniment to the rest of the meal.

1 carrot, roughly grated

100 g (3½ oz) packet rocket

½ small red onion, finely sliced

15 g (½ oz) fresh mint, chopped

50 g (2 oz) shelled pistachios, roughly chopped

For the dressing:

juice of ½ lemon

4 tablespoons olive oil

1 teaspoon ground cinnamon

chicken with lemon and olives

SERVES 6 • PREP 10 MINS • COOK 30 MINS • CALS PER PORTION 250 • FAT PER PORTION 12 G

2 tablespoons olive oil

6 chicken breasts

1 onion, thinly sliced

2 garlic cloves, crushed

1 large pinch of saffron strands, crushed, or ¼ teaspoon ground saffron

450 ml (¾ pint) boiling chicken stock

1 preserved lemon, cubed (see tip below)

1 cinnamon stick

juice of ½ lemon

125 g (4 oz) brown or green olives

15 g (½ oz) fresh coriander, roughly chopped

Tip

Preserved lemons, a main ingredient in Moroccan cooking, are available in some supermarkets. If you cannot find the lemons, place the grated zest of 1 unwaxed lemon, 2 tablespoons water, 1 tablespoon olive oil and 1 tablespoon sea salt in a small saucepan. Bring to the boil and simmer gently for 5 minutes. Use the zest and the poaching syrup in place of 1 preserved lemon.

1 Heat the oil in a large pan. Add the chicken and brown for 5 minutes, turning once. Transfer to a plate and set aside.
2 Add the sliced onion to the pan, cook gently for 5 minutes until softened. Add the garlic and the saffron and cook for 1 minute. Return the chicken to the pan and pour in the stock. Add the preserved lemon, cinnamon stick and lemon juice. Cover and simmer for 15 minutes, until the chicken is cooked.
3 Remove the chicken from the pan and keep warm in a serving dish. Add the olives to the pan and increase the heat, bringing the sauce to a boil. Simmer for 5 minutes to thicken. Stir in the fresh coriander and spoon the sauce over the chicken.

saffron couscous

SERVES 6 • PREP 5 MINS • COOK 5 MINS, PLUS STANDING • CALS PER PORTION 190 • FAT PER PORTION 7 G

1 In a saucepan, bring the stock to the boil with the saffron. Turn off the heat and allow to stand for 2 minutes so that the flavour and colour of the saffron is released into the stock.
2 Bring the stock back to the boil. Turn off the heat and add the couscous. Stir well and cover for 5 minutes.
3 The couscous should now be cooked and fluffy, with all the water absorbed. Gently but thoroughly fold in the remaining ingredients until the butter has melted. Serve immediately.

Tips
The saffron can be replaced with 1 teaspoon of turmeric – the flavour won't be identical but you will achieve a lovely golden colour. For a stunning presentation, pack the cooked couscous into a bowl, then turn it out onto your serving plate and decorate with chopped herbs and saffron threads.

500 ml (17 fl oz) vegetable stock

1 large pinch of saffron strands, crushed, or ¼ tablespoon ground saffron

300 g (11 oz) couscous

50 g (2 oz) toasted flaked almonds

15 g (½ oz) fresh flat leaf parsley, chopped

15 g (½ oz) butter

orange salad with cinnamon

SERVES 6 • PREP 10 MINS • COOK NONE • CALS PER PORTION 60 • FAT PER PORTION 0 G

1 Peel the oranges and thickly slice. Arrange the slices on a serving dish and drizzle with the orange blossom water.
2 Sprinkle with the ground cinnamon and icing sugar, and garnish with mint leaves and cinnamon sticks to serve.

4 large oranges

2 tablespoons orange blossom water (optional)

1 teaspoon ground cinnamon

15 g (½ oz) icing sugar

fresh mint leaves and cinnamon sticks, to garnish

spiced vegetable and chickpea tagine

SERVES 6 • PREP 10 MINS • COOK 25–30 MINS • CALS PER PORTION 250 • FAT PER PORTION 6 G

2 tablespoons olive oil

1 red onion, thinly sliced

2 garlic cloves, crushed

½ teaspoon ground cumin

1 tablespoon harissa

225 g (8 oz) dried apricots, roughly chopped

2 tomatoes, roughly chopped

2 large courgettes, thickly sliced

1 red pepper, cored, deseeded and cubed

1 aubergine, trimmed and cubed

300 ml (½ pint) boiling vegetable stock

410 g (approx 14 oz) can chickpeas, drained

15 g (½ oz) fresh flat leaf parsley

1 In a large saucepan, gently heat the oil and add the sliced onion. Cook for 5 minutes until softened. Add the garlic, cumin and harissa and cook for a further 1 minute.

2 Add the apricots and all the vegetables to the pan and stir. Pour over the stock and bring to the boil. Simmer covered for 15 minutes, then add the chickpeas and cook for a further 10 minutes, or until the vegetables are cooked. Season with salt and black pepper, sprinkle over the parsley and serve.

Tip

If you can't find ready-made harissa paste, put 1 roasted, skinned red pepper, 1 sliced red chilli, 1 teaspoon crushed coriander and 4 tablespoons olive oil into a food processor and whizz until combined.

savoury mushroom starter

SERVES 4 • PREP 10 MINS • COOK 5 MINS • CALS PER PORTION 150 • FAT PER PORTION 8 G

1 Trim the stems of the mushrooms, rinse them quickly under cold water and wipe clean with kitchen paper.
2 Mix the flour and curry powder in a small bowl and dust each mushroom cap with some of the mixture, shaking off any excess.
3 Heat a wok or a large frying pan over a high heat until hot. Add the oil and when slightly smoking, add the mushrooms. Slowly pan-fry them for 2 minutes on either side. Garnish with chopped chillies and serve immediately.

225 g (8 oz) fresh shiitake or brown cap mushrooms

2 tablespoons plain flour

1 tablespoon madras curry powder

3 tablespoons groundnut oil

1 green chilli, deseeded and finely chopped

1 red chilli, deseeded and finely chopped

egg-fried rice

SERVES 4 • PREP 5 MINS • COOK 8 MINS • CALS PER PORTION 300 • FAT PER PORTION 4 G

1 Put the eggs, sesame oil and salt in a small jug or bowl, mix with a fork and set aside.
2 Heat a wok over a high heat. Add the groundnut oil and, when it's very hot and slightly smoking, add the cold, cooked rice. Stir-fry for 2 minutes, or until thoroughly heated through.
3 Drizzle in the egg and oil mixture, and stir-fry for 2–3 minutes or until the eggs have set and the mixture is dry. Season with ground black pepper and serve.

Tip
Make sure that the rice is very cold and the wok very hot, as this stops the rice becoming greasy.

2 eggs, lightly beaten

2 teaspoons sesame oil

½ teaspoon salt

2 tablespoons groundnut oil

250 g (9 oz) long-grain rice, cooked and chilled

stir-fried vegetables with peanuts

SERVES 4 • PREP 5 MINS • COOK 7 MINS • CALS PER PORTION 180 • FAT PER PORTION 11 G

1 Heat a wok or large frying pan over a high heat until hot. Add the oil. When very hot and slightly smoking add the vegetables, garlic and chillies. Stir-fry for 1 minute.

2 Add the fish or soy sauce, rice wine or sherry, lime juice and sugar. Season with ground black pepper to taste. Stir-fry for 5 minutes, stirring constantly.

3 Add the peanuts, cook for 1 minute and serve immediately, with cooked noodles if desired.

2 tablespoons groundnut oil

2 x 450 g (1 lb) packets ready-prepared stir-fry vegetables

2 tablespoons chopped garlic

3 red or green chillies, deseeded and finely chopped

4 tablespoons fish sauce or light soy sauce

1 tablespoon rice wine or dry sherry

2 tablespoons lime juice

2 teaspoons sugar

3 tablespoons roasted peanuts, roughly chopped

cooked egg noodles (optional)

pork with pineapple

SERVES 4 • PREP 10 MINS • COOK 8 MINS • CALS PER PORTION 240 • FAT PER PORTION 11 G

1 Place the strips of pork in a shallow dish. Mix 1 tablespoon soy sauce with the rice wine or sherry, the sesame oil and cornflour, and pour over the pork. Mix well to coat the pieces.
2 Heat a wok over a high heat until very hot. Add the vegetable oil and, when it's slightly smoking, add the garlic and stir-fry for 30 seconds.
3 Add the strips of pork to the wok and stir-fry for 3 minutes. Add the cubes of pineapple, the sugar, the remaining soy sauce and the spring onions, and stir-fry for 3 minutes. Season with ground black pepper and serve.

450 g (1 lb) pork fillet, cut into thin strips about 5 cm (2 in) long

2 tablespoons soy sauce

2 teaspoons rice wine or dry sherry

1 teaspoon sesame oil

2 teaspoons cornflour

1 tablespoon vegetable oil

3 garlic cloves, roughly chopped

225 g (8 oz) fresh or canned pineapple, cut into 2.5 cm (1 in) cubes

2 teaspoons sugar

2 spring onions, finely sliced

sweet ginger chicken

SERVES 4 • PREP 10 MINS, PLUS MARINATING • COOK 20 MINS • CALS PER PORTION 245 • FAT PER PORTION 10 G

450 g (1 lb) skinless, boneless chicken thighs

3 teaspoons light soy sauce

3 tablespoons dry sherry or rice wine

3 teaspoons sesame oil

2 teaspoons cornflour

1 tablespoon vegetable oil

3 tablespoons chopped fresh root ginger

2 tablespoons dark soy sauce

2 tablespoons sugar

150 ml (¼ pint) chicken stock

2 spring onions, finely sliced

1 tablespoon fresh coriander, roughly chopped

1 Preheat the oven to gas mark 9/240°C (475°F). Cut the chicken into 5 cm (2 in) chunks.

2 Mix the light soy sauce with 1 tablespoon of the sherry or rice wine, 1 teaspoon sesame oil, the cornflour, and salt and pepper. Pour over the chicken. Mix to coat the chicken pieces, then leave to marinate for 30 minutes. Drain and discard the marinade.

3 Put the chicken in a roasting tin, mix the remaining sesame oil with the vegetable oil and drizzle over the chicken. Place in the oven and cook for 15 minutes or until golden. Remove from the oven and leave the chicken to drain on kitchen paper.

4 Heat a wok or large frying pan over a high heat until hot. Add the ginger and dry-fry it for 1 minute until crispy. Add the dark soy sauce, sugar, a little freshly ground black pepper and the chicken stock, and continue to stir-fry for 1 minute. Reduce the heat, cover the pan and simmer for a further 8 minutes.

5 Uncover the pan and cook the sauce until reduced by half. Add the remaining rice wine or sherry and cook for 2 minutes more. Add the chicken and cook for a further 3–4 minutes or until hot. Sprinkle over the spring onions and coriander, and serve.

leg of lamb with anchovies
and redcurrant gravy

SERVES 8 • PREP 25 MINS • COOK 2 HRS 30 MINS, PLUS RESTING • CALS PER PORTION 337 • FAT PER PORTION 19 G

1 Preheat the oven to gas mark 6/200°C (400°F). With a sharp knife, make 12 deep incisions in the fleshy side of the leg of lamb.
2 Cut 3 of the garlic cloves into quarters. Divide the rosemary sprigs and anchovies into 12. Insert a piece of rosemary, garlic and anchovy into each incision in the lamb.
3 Crush the remaining garlic, mix it into the butter with the mustard and 1 teaspoon chopped rosemary, then spread over the lamb. Put the meat in a large roasting tin and cook according to the chart, below right. When cooked, remove the lamb from the tin and cover with foil. Leave to rest for 15–20 minutes before carving.
4 To make the gravy, skim off the fat from the sediment in the roasting tin. Set the tin on the hob. Whisk the flour into the roasting tin until it forms a smooth paste, then blend in the red wine and bring to the boil. Bubble for 2 minutes. Pour in the lamb stock and redcurrant jelly, and continue to cook over a high heat for 3–5 minutes. Strain into a gravy boat and serve immediately with the lamb.

2.7 kg (6 lb) leg of lamb

5 large garlic cloves, peeled

3 sprigs of fresh rosemary, plus 1 teaspoon chopped

50 g (2 oz) can anchovies, drained

50 g (2 oz) soft unsalted butter

2 tablespoons Dijon mustard

For the redcurrant gravy:

2 tablespoons flour

150 ml (¼ pint) red wine

600 ml (1 pint) lamb stock

2 tablespoons redcurrant jelly

Lamb roasting chart
rare
20 mins per 500 g (1 lb 2 oz), plus 20 mins
medium
25 mins per 500 g (1 lb 2 oz), plus 25 mins
well done
30 mins per 500 g (1 lb 2 oz), plus 30 mins

roasted ratatouille

SERVES 8 • PREP 20 MINS • COOK 40 MINS • CALS PER PORTION 180 • FAT PER PORTION 14 G

1 Preheat the oven to gas mark 6/200°C (400°F). Put the peppers, aubergines, onions, courgettes, tomatoes and garlic in a large roasting tin.
2 Sprinkle the fennel seeds over the vegetables. Pour over the olive oil, add the fresh thyme and season with salt and pepper.
3 Put the tin in the oven and roast for 40 minutes, tossing the mixture halfway through, until tender and slightly charred.

400 g (14 oz) red peppers, cored, deseeded and roughly chopped into chunks

400 g (14 oz) aubergines, trimmed and cut into chunks

400 g (14 oz) red onions, peeled and cut into wedges

400 g (14 oz) courgettes, thickly sliced

250 g (9 oz) cherry tomatoes

4–5 garlic cloves, unpeeled

1 teaspoon fennel seeds

150 ml (¼ pint) olive oil

4 sprigs of fresh thyme

olive oil mash with olives and mint

SERVES 8 • PREP 15 MINS • COOK 25 MINS • CALS PER PORTION 352 • FAT PER PORTION 18 G

2 kg (4½ lb) potatoes

150 ml (¼ pint) double cream

6 tablespoons olive oil

75 g (3 oz) pitted black olives, roughly chopped

4 tablespoons coarsely chopped fresh mint

1 Peel and halve the potatoes. Boil in salted water until tender.
2 Drain the potatoes and return to the pan over a gentle heat for 1 minute, shaking it continuously to remove any excess water.
3 Add the cream and olive oil to the pan and mash well with a fork or a potato masher. Fold in the olives and mint, season with salt and pepper, and serve.

ham and lentil crostinis

SERVES 6 • PREP 5 MINS • COOK 10 MINS • CALS PER PORTION 170 • FAT PER PORTION 4.5 G

1 Preheat the oven to gas mark 6/200°C (400°F). Brush the sliced rounds of bread with the olive oil on both sides and bake for about 5 minutes until golden.

2 In a bowl, mix together the lentils, mustard, white wine vinegar and parsley. Spoon onto the circles of toasted bread and top with slices of Parma ham.

1 baguette, sliced into 5 mm (¼ in) slices

1 tablespoon olive oil

450 g (1 lb) can green lentils, drained and rinsed

2 teaspoons Dijon mustard

1 teaspoon white wine vinegar

1 small bunch of flat leaf parsley, chopped

80 g (approx 3 oz) packet Parma ham

poussin with lemon and thyme

SERVES 6 • PREP 15 MINS • COOK 45 MINS • CALS PER PORTION 500 • FAT PER PORTION 26 G

4 lemons

3 poussins

3 teaspoons tapenade

1 bunch of fresh thyme

2 red onions, peeled and cut into wedges

1.1 kg (2½ lb) new potatoes, roughly chopped

3 whole heads of garlic

150 ml (¼ pint) olive oil

1 Heat the oven to gas mark 6/200°C (400°F). Slice 1 lemon and cut the other 3 into quarters.
2 Using two fingers, gently loosen the skin from the neck of each poussin. Spread a little tapenade under the skin with a slice of lemon and then insert a few sprigs of thyme into each poussin's cavity.
3 Place the poussins in a casserole dish. Surround them with the rest of thyme, the wedges of lemon and onion, the potatoes and the garlic. Drizzle with the oil and season well.
4 Place the casserole in the oven and roast for 40–50 minutes until the poussins are cooked through.

summer fruit clafoutis

SERVES 6 • PREP 10 MINS • COOK 15 MINS • CALS PER PORTION 135 • FAT PER PORTION 9 G

450 g (1 lb) fresh or frozen mixed summer fruits (raspberries, strawberries, blackberries and blueberries)

3 tablespoons sugar

2 eggs

6 tablespoons double cream

6 tablespoons milk

1 Preheat the oven to gas mark 6/200°C (400°F). If using frozen fruit, defrost it and drain thoroughly. Put all fruit into an ovenproof dish and sprinkle with half of the sugar.
2 Whisk the eggs for 2 minutes until frothy, add the remaining sugar and whisk for another 2 minutes. Add the cream and milk and beat until well blended.
3 Pour the mixture over the fruit and bake for 15 minutes, until the batter is golden and set.

broccoli, boursin and olive pizzas
with sweet and sour peppers

SERVES 4 • PREP 10 MINS • COOK 5 MINS • CALS PER PORTION 500 • FAT PER PORTION 33 G

1 First make the sweet and sour peppers. Heat the olive oil in a large frying pan and fry the garlic for a few minutes until golden. Add the yellow, red and green pepper strips, the caster sugar and the white wine vinegar. Fry for 5 minutes, then keep warm.
2 Meanwhile, plunge the broccoli florets into a saucepan of boiling, salted water for 5 minutes, drain, then plunge into cold water and drain again.
3 Cut the loaf of ciabatta in half, then slice down the middle horizontally to make four pieces. Top each quarter with a little garlic and herb cheese, the broccoli and olives. Season with salt and ground black pepper and drizzle over the olive oil.
4 Place the pizzas under a hot grill for 5 minutes until the cheese has melted and the ciabatta is brown. Serve with the rocket and the warm sweet and sour peppers.

2 x 200 g (7 oz) packets ready-to-cook broccoli florets

1 small ciabatta

2 x 80 g (approx 3 oz) packets soft cheese with garlic and herbs

16 kalamata olives, pitted and roughly chopped

4 tablespoons olive oil

50 g (2 oz) rocket

For the sweet and sour peppers:

1 tablespoon olive oil

1 garlic clove, crushed

1 yellow pepper, 1 red pepper and 1 green pepper, cored, deseeded and cut into strips

1 teaspoon caster sugar

3 tablespoons white wine vinegar

banoffee crumble

SERVES 4 • PREP 5 MINS • COOK 5 MINS • CALS PER PORTION 570 • FAT PER PORTION 25 G

150 g (5 oz) butter

125 g (4 oz) muesli

4 tablespoons brown sugar

4 bananas, sliced

8 tablespoons toffee sauce

1 In a large saucepan, melt 50 g (2 oz) butter over a low heat. Remove the pan from the heat, add the muesli and stir to coat evenly and thoroughly.

2 In a large frying pan, melt the remaining butter. Add the sugar, stirring until dissolved. Then add the bananas and fry for 5 minutes until golden all over.

3 Divide the slices of banana between 4 dessert bowls, top each with 2 tablespoons of toffee sauce and sprinkle over the muesli. Place under a hot grill for 2 minutes, then serve.

pan-fried turkey wrapped in ham
with white bean mash

SERVES 4 • PREP 5 MINS • COOK 15 MINS • CALS PER PORTION 600 • FAT PER PORTION 23 G

1 Put 2 sprigs of rosemary on top of each turkey steak, then wrap 3 slices of ham around each to secure the rosemary.
2 In a large frying pan, heat the oil and fry the whole garlic cloves for a few minutes until golden. Add the turkey steaks and pan-fry over a medium heat for 10 minutes, turning after 5 minutes, until cooked.
3 Meanwhile, for the mash, put the cannellini beans, milk, chopped thyme and olive oil in a large saucepan. Bring to the boil then simmer gently for 10 minutes until the liquid has thickened. Mash the beans and season with salt and pepper.
4 Serve the white bean mash with the turkey, accompanied by a tomato and flat leaf parsley salad if desired.

8 sprigs of fresh rosemary

4 large turkey breast steaks

12 slices Black Forest ham

2 tablespoons olive oil

3 garlic cloves, peeled

tomato salad, garnished with flat leaf parsley (optional)

For the white bean mash:

2 x 410 g (approx 14 oz) cans cannellini beans, drained and rinsed

150 ml (¼ pint) full-fat milk

2 tablespoons chopped fresh thyme

4 tablespoons olive oil

coffee and chocolate trifles

SERVES 4 • PREP 10 MINS • COOK NONE • CALS PER PORTION 660
• FAT PER PORTION 70 G

1 tablespoon instant coffee

500 g (1 lb 2 oz) tub mascarpone

4 chocolate brownies

2 tablespoons rum (optional)

4 tablespoons crème fraîche

2 tablespoons toasted flaked almonds

2 teaspoons ground cinnamon

1 Dissolve the instant coffee in 75 ml (3 fl oz) boiling water. In a large bowl, mix together the mascarpone and the coffee liquid until combined.
2 Cut the brownies into small cubes and arrange the pieces in the bottom of four 250 ml (8 fl oz) tumblers. Pour the rum, if using, over the top.
3 Top the brownies with the coffee mascarpone to the rim of each glass. Finish each with a dollop of crème fraîche, a sprinkling of flaked almonds and a dusting of cinnamon. Chill until required.

basque-style mussel stew
with green chillies, peppers and tomatoes

SERVES 4 • PREP 10 MINS • COOK 15 MINS • CALS PER PORTION 210 • FAT PER PORTION 10 G

1 Heat the oil in a large pan or wok and fry the onions gently for 5 minutes. Increase the heat and add the chillies and peppers. Stir-fry for 2–3 minutes.

2 Add the cherry tomatoes and cook for 1 minute. Add the paprika, stir well, then pour in the creamed tomatoes or passata. Bring to the boil, add the mussels and cover.

3 Simmer for 5 minutes, then remove the lid, stir well and season with salt and ground black pepper. Serve with lemon wedges and crusty French bread if desired.

3 tablespoons olive oil

2 small onions, finely sliced

2 large green chillies, finely sliced

2 red peppers, cored, deseeded and finely sliced

250 g (9 oz) cherry tomatoes, halved

2 teaspoons paprika

200 ml (7 fl oz) creamed tomatoes or passata

2 x 500 g (1 lb 2 oz) packets ready-cooked mussels

marinated pork
with horseradish and watercress mash

SERVES 4 • PREP 10 MINS, PLUS CHILLING • COOK 30 MINS • CALS PER PORTION 660 • FAT PER PORTION 33 G

4 large pork loin chops

250 ml (8 fl oz) bottle Italian salad dressing

For the mash:

750 g (1 lb 10 oz) potatoes, peeled and cut into even chunks

85 g (approx 3¼ oz) packet watercress, thick stalks removed

3 teaspoons creamed horseradish

1 In a shallow dish, coat the pork chops in the dressing. Cover and chill to marinate for 30 minutes. Place under a hot grill for 30 minutes, turning halfway, until cooked and crispy.
2 Meanwhile, put the potatoes in a large saucepan of cold, salted water. Bring to the boil, then cover and simmer for 20 minutes. Drain and mash until creamy. Fold in the watercress and horseradish, season with salt and black pepper, and serve with the pork chops.

sugar-roasted plums with cream

SERVES 4 • PREP 5 MINS • COOK 20 MINS • CALS PER PORTION 420 • FAT PER PORTION 30 G

12 small purple plums

4 tablespoons caster sugar

3 tablespoons liqueur, such as kirsch, Cointreau or brandy

½ teaspoon vanilla extract

250 ml (8 fl oz) extra thick double cream

4 shortbread biscuits

1 Preheat the oven to gas mark 7/220°C (425°F). Make a small slit along the natural line on each plum. Place the plums in a roasting tin with the sugar, liqueur and vanilla extract. Bake for 15 minutes.
2 Remove from the oven – the plums should be sticky and browned. Add 2 tablespoons water to the tin and return to the oven for 5 minutes.
3 Serve the plums with their juices from the tin, a dollop of cream and the biscuits.

low-fat food

Keeping your cupboards stocked full of handy ingredients will make low-fat cooking a breeze! From pasta to pulses, you'll find it easy to throw together a quick and healthy supper if you can reach for some tasty standbys. See page 11 for a list of essential low-fat ingredients.

LOW-FAT DRESSINGS
balsamic vinaigrette

50 ml (2 fl oz) balsamic vinegar

125 ml (4 fl oz) cold chicken or vegetable stock

¼ teaspoon mild paprika

1 teaspoon dried mixed herbs

2 tablespoons reduced-calorie tomato ketchup

CALS PER 2 TBSP (30 ML) 16 •
FAT PER 2 TBSP (30 ML) .2 G

Put all the ingredients in a small screw-top jar and shake until well combined.

creamy italian dressing

50 g (2 oz) low-fat plain yogurt

50 ml (2 fl oz) low-fat mayonnaise

50 ml (2 fl oz) skimmed milk

½ teaspoon dried Italian seasoning

¼ teaspoon garlic powder

CALS PER 2 TBSP (30 ML) 56 •
FAT PER 2 TBSP (30 ML) 3 G

In a small bowl, stir together the yogurt, mayonnaise and skimmed milk. Add the dried Italian seasoning and garlic powder and stir to combine.

tomato vinaigrette

125 g (4 oz) canned, chopped tomatoes

2 tablespoons white wine vinegar

½ teaspoon dried basil

½ teaspoon dried thyme

¼ teaspoon Dijon mustard

CALS PER 2 TBSP (30 ML) 7 •
FAT PER 2 TBSP (30 ML) .2 G

Put all the ingredients in a food processor. Whizz for about 20 seconds until smooth. Pour into a jar and shake well before serving.

thousand island dressing

250 ml (8 fl oz) tomato ketchup

250 ml (8 fl oz) low-fat yogurt

125 ml (4 fl oz) white wine vinegar

2 tablespoons sugar

½ teaspoon ready-made English mustard

CALS PER 2 TBSP (30 ML) 15 •
FAT PER 2 TBSP (30 ML) .4 G

Put all the ingredients in a bowl. Blend together until very smooth.

creamy blue cheese dressing

Put all the ingredients in a food processor. Blend for a few seconds, allowing the blue cheese to remain slightly chunky.

CALS PER 2 TBSP (30 ML) 26 •
FAT PER 2 TBSP (30 ML) 1 G

225 g (8 oz) low-fat cottage cheese

2 tablespoons blue cheese, crumbled

2 tablespoons skimmed milk

1 garlic clove, roughly chopped

lean paprika meatballs

SERVES 6 • PREP 15 MINS • COOK 6–8 MINS • CALS PER PORTION 160 • FAT PER PORTION 9 G

1 Preheat the grill to its highest setting. Line the grill tray with foil and spray it with low-fat cooking spray.
2 In a large bowl combine the minced beef with the aubergine, lemon juice, paprika, a pinch of salt and ground black pepper. Using your hands, form the mixture into little balls – about 30.
3 Space the meatballs on the grill rack and grill for 3–4 minutes on each side. Serve them piping hot, with flat noodles and a fresh tomato sauce if desired.

low-fat cooking spray

500 g (1 lb 2 oz) extra lean minced beef

1 large aubergine, roasted and peeled

juice of ½ lemon

1 tablespoon paprika

sesame meatballs and vegetable noodles

SERVES 4 • PREP 10 MINS • COOK 15 MINS • CALS PER PORTION 210 • FAT PER PORTION 11 G

240 g (8½ oz) minced pork
or beef

2 tablespoons fresh wholemeal
breadcrumbs

1 egg, beaten

1 tablespoon light soy sauce

1 tablespoon sesame seeds

1 garlic clove, crushed

1 tablespoon vegetable oil

2 carrots, peeled

2 courgettes, trimmed

1 Mix together the minced meat, breadcrumbs, egg, soy sauce, sesame seeds and garlic. Season with salt and black pepper. Using wet hands, shape the mixture into walnut-sized meatballs.
2 Heat the oil in a frying pan and cook the meatballs over a medium heat, turning frequently so that they are cooked evenly. Remove with a slotted spoon and keep warm.
3 Using a potato peeler, shred the carrots and courgettes into wide ribbons. Add these to the pan with 2 tablespoons water and stir-fry for 5 minutes.
4 Arrange the vegetable 'noodles' on warmed plates and spoon the meatballs on top. Serve, with egg noodles if desired.

oriental chicken stir-fry

SERVES 4 • PREP 15 MINS • COOK 10 MINS • CALS PER PORTION 160 • FAT PER PORTION 10 G

1 Heat the oil in a wok or large frying pan. Add the cashew nuts and stir-fry for about 1 minute until browned. Lift them out with a slotted spoon and drain on kitchen paper.
2 Add the spring onions, peppers, carrot, cauliflower, baby sweetcorn and strips of chicken to the pan. Stir-fry over a high heat for 4–5 minutes until the chicken is cooked, yet the vegetables remain crisp and colourful.
3 Stir the whole mushrooms into the pan, then add the ginger, five-spice powder and fresh coriander. Cook for 2 minutes more. Add the soy sauce and season with salt and ground black pepper.
4 Serve the stir-fry on warmed plates, sprinkled with the cashew nuts and garnished with sprigs of fresh coriander.

1 tablespoon sesame or vegetable oil

25 g (1 oz) cashew nuts

1 bunch of spring onions, sliced

1 green pepper and 1 red pepper, cored, deseeded and finely sliced

1 large carrot, cut into matchsticks

125 g (4 oz) cauliflower, broken into small florets

100 g (3 oz) baby sweetcorn, sliced lengthways

350 g (12 oz) skinless, boneless chicken, sliced into strips

240 g (8½ oz) oyster or button mushrooms

1 teaspoon finely grated fresh root ginger or ½ teaspoon ground

1 teaspoon Chinese five-spice powder

1 tablespoon chopped fresh coriander

1 tablespoon light soy sauce

chicken pizzaiola

SERVES 2 • PREP 10 MINS • COOK 15 MINS • CALS PER PORTION 350 • FAT PER PORTION 6 G

1 Microwave the potato on HIGH for 8–10 minutes.

2 Meanwhile, spray a frying pan with low-fat cooking spray and heat the pan. Add the strips of chicken and red pepper. Cook until lightly browned, then add the garlic and mushrooms, and cook for a further 2 minutes.

3 Chop the tomatoes slightly and add to the pan with their juices, the dried herbs and the olives. Simmer for 5 minutes. Season with salt and ground black pepper and serve each portion with half the potato.

1 baking potato

low-fat cooking spray

125 g (4 oz) chicken breast, cut into strips

1 red pepper, cored, deseeded and cut into strips

1 garlic clove, chopped

100 g (3½ oz) mushrooms, sliced

200 g (7 oz) can tomatoes

1 teaspoon dried mixed herbs

6 pitted olives

parmesan chicken with tomatoes and courgettes

SERVES 4 • PREP 30 MINS • COOK 30 MINS • CALS PER PORTION 300 • FAT PER PORTION 14 G

1 Preheat the oven to gas mark 6/200°C (400°F). Sprinkle the flour on a plate, season with salt and ground black pepper and use it to coat the chicken breasts.
2 In a bowl mix together the dried breadcrumbs, cheese and herbs. Dip each chicken breast into the beaten egg, then coat with the breadcrumb mixture.
3 Place the chicken breasts in an ovenproof dish and cook in the oven for 25–30 minutes, or until the juices run clear.
4 Meanwhile, heat the oil in a pan. Lightly sauté the onion for 3 minutes, then add the tomatoes, courgette and basil, cooking over a very low heat for 10 minutes. Serve with the chicken.

25 g (1 oz) plain flour

4 x 150 g (5 oz) skinless, boneless chicken breasts, rinsed

25 g (1 oz) dried breadcrumbs

25 g (1 oz) Parmesan, finely grated

1 teaspoon dried mixed Italian herbs

1 egg, beaten

4 teaspoons olive oil

1 onion, chopped

4 tomatoes, quartered

1 courgette, sliced

1 tablespoon chopped fresh basil

chicken kiev

SERVES 4 • PREP 15 MINS • COOK 25 MINS • CALS PER PORTION 310 • FAT PER PORTION 5 G

4 x 175 g (6 oz) skinless chicken breasts

100 g (3½ oz) low-fat cream cheese

1 tablespoon fresh breadcrumbs

1 egg, separated

1 garlic clove, crushed

2 tablespoons chopped fresh parsley

200 g (7 oz) fine dried breadcrumbs

2 teaspoons paprika

plain white flour, for dusting

1 Preheat the oven to gas mark 7/220°C (425°F). Cut a deep slit lengthways in each chicken breast.

2 In a bowl mix together the cream cheese, fresh breadcrumbs, egg yolk, garlic and chopped parsley and season with ground black pepper. Spoon the mixture into the slits in the chicken breasts then, using wooden cocktail sticks, secure the pockets.

3 Lightly beat the egg white. Spread the dried breadcrumbs and paprika on a flat plate. Dip each chicken breast in a little plain white flour. Brush with egg white, then press on the breadcrumbs until the chicken is well coated.

4 Place the chicken on a baking tray and bake in the oven for 25 minutes. Serve, with a green salad if desired.

pasta with green beans
and sun-dried tomatoes

SERVES 2 • PREP 5 MINS • COOK 10 MINS • CALS PER PORTION 560 • FAT PER PORTION 20 G

1 Cook the pasta in a large saucepan of boiling, salted water according to packet instructions.
2 Meanwhile, steam or boil the fine green beans for 5 minutes until cooked.
3 Drain the pasta, return it to the pan and add the cooked green beans, pesto and soft cheese, stirring well to mix.
4 Add the sun-dried tomatoes, then season with salt and black pepper. Serve with fresh basil leaves scattered over the top.

175 g (6 oz) pasta shapes

175 g (6 oz) fine green beans, sliced

1 tablespoon green pesto

75 g (3 oz) low-fat soft cheese

50 g (2 oz) sun-dried tomatoes, rinsed and patted dry

fresh basil leaves, to garnish

tuna pizza

SERVES 2 • PREP 5 MINS • COOK 15 MINS, PLUS SAUCE-MAKING • CALS PER PORTION 270 • FAT PER PORTION 7 G

1 medium size thin and crispy pizza base

3 tablespoons basic tomato sauce (see below)

1 small onion, sliced

50 g (2 oz) mushrooms, sliced

100 g (3½ oz) can tuna in brine, drained and flaked

25 g (1 oz) sweetcorn kernels

40 g (1½ oz) half-fat mozzarella cheese, cubed

For the tomato sauce:

400 g (14 oz) can chopped tomatoes

2 garlic cloves, crushed

3 teaspoons artificial sweetener

grated zest of ½ lemon

2 tablespoons chopped fresh parsley

Tip
The tomato sauce can be made in advance and stored in the fridge.

1 To make the tomato sauce, put all the ingredients except the parsley in a saucepan and bring to the boil. Reduce the heat and simmer, uncovered, for 45 minutes, until the sauce is thick. Add the parsley and leave to cool.
2 Preheat the oven to gas mark 7/220°C (425°F). Spread the pizza base with 3 tablespoons of the basic tomato sauce. Top with the onion, mushrooms, tuna, sweetcorn and mozzarella. Season with salt and ground black pepper.
3 Place in the oven and bake for 25 minutes until crisp.

glazed salmon fillets

SERVES 1 • PREP 5 MINS • COOK 6–8 MINS • CALS PER PORTION 285 • FAT PER PORTION 21 G

1 Preheat the grill to medium. Place the salmon fillet, skin side up, on the grill rack. Mix together the remaining ingredients and use to coat the skin.

2 Grill the fish for 6–8 minutes until the flesh is cooked, and the skin is blackened and crisp.

175 g (6 oz) salmon fillet, with skin

¼ teaspoon mild chilli powder

¼ teaspoon soft brown sugar

¼ teaspoon white wine vinegar

cheesy baked cod

SERVES 2 • PREP 10 MINS • COOK 20 MINUTES • CALS PER PORTION 290 • FAT PER PORTION 7 G

1 Preheat the oven to gas mark 4/180°C (350°F). Arrange the cod fillets, side by side, in a shallow ovenproof dish. Season well with salt and ground black pepper, and sprinkle over the herbs.
2 In a small bowl mix together the fromage frais, spring onions and all but 1 tablespoon of the grated cheese. Season to taste, then spoon the mixture over the sliced tomatoes.
3 Place the fish in the oven and bake for 10 minutes, then place the tomato mixture on top of the fish and sprinkle the remaining cheese on top. Cook for another 10 minutes, until golden.
4 Garnish with lemon twists and serve.

2 x 125 g (4 oz) cod fillets, skinned and boned

pinch of dried mixed herbs

125 g (4 oz) low-fat plain fromage frais

2 spring onions, chopped

75 g (3 oz) half-fat cheddar, grated

2 tomatoes, sliced

2 lemon twists, to garnish

tomato and tuna pasta bake

SERVES 4 • PREP 5 MINS • COOK 30 MINS • CALS PER PORTION 490 • FAT PER PORTION 21 G

1 Preheat the oven to gas mark 5/190°C (375°F). Heat the oil and gently fry the onion and garlic until soft.
2 Stir in the tuna, the canned and sun-dried tomatoes, and the white wine. Cover and simmer gently.
3 Meanwhile cook the pasta in a large saucepan of boiling, lightly salted water for 5 minutes less than the time recommended on the packet instructions. Drain well.
4 Stir the cooked pasta into the tomato and tuna sauce, season to taste with salt and ground black pepper then pour the mixture into an ovenproof dish.
5 Sprinkle with the grated cheese and breadcrumbs and bake in the oven for 15 minutes, or until the top is crunchy.

1 tablespoon olive oil

1 onion, finely chopped

2 garlic cloves, crushed

100 g (3½ oz) can tuna in brine, drained and flaked

400 g (14 oz) can chopped tomatoes

125 g (4 oz) sun-dried tomatoes in oil, drained and chopped

150 ml (¼ pint) white wine

240 g (8½ oz) pasta shapes

1 tablespoon half-fat cheddar, finely grated

1 tablespoon fresh breadcrumbs

scrambled egg on toast

SERVES 1 • PREP 2 MINS • COOK 5 MINS • CALS PER PORTION 200 • FAT PER PORTION 9 G

1 Beat the egg with the milk and season with a little salt and freshly ground black pepper.
2 Spray a non-stick pan with a little of the low-fat cooking spray and heat the pan. Pour in the egg and milk mixture and stir with a wooden spoon over a gentle heat until set.
3 Serve the scrambled egg with grilled tomato and hot toast. Garnish with snipped chives.

1 egg

1 tablespoon skimmed milk

low-fat cooking spray

1 grilled tomato

1 slice of wholemeal toast

snipped fresh chives, to garnish

winter vegetable hot pot

SERVES 4 • PREP 10 MINS • COOK 1 HR • CALS PER PORTION 325 • FAT PER PORTION 4 G

2 onions, sliced

2 leeks, cleaned and sliced

2 carrots, peeled and cut into matchsticks

1 parsnip, peeled and cubed

2 celery sticks, sliced

1 small swede, peeled and cubed

50 g (2 oz) flour, seasoned

600 ml (1 pint) vegetable stock

1 teaspoon yeast extract

1 tablespoon tomato purée

1 teaspoon dried mixed herbs

700 g (1½ lb) potatoes, peeled and thinly sliced

1 tablespoon vegetable oil

1 Preheat the oven to gas mark 4/180°C (350°F). Mix together all the prepared vegetables except the potatoes and toss them in the seasoned flour. Put in an ovenproof dish or casserole.

2 Mix together the stock, yeast extract, tomato purée and herbs and pour over the vegetables. Arrange the potato slices on top, overlapping them if necessary.

3 Brush the potato slices with the oil and cover the dish before placing it in the middle of the oven.

4 After 45 minutes remove the lid and transfer the dish to the top shelf of the oven for about 15 minutes, until the potatoes are crisp and brown.

garlic mashed potato

SERVES 4 • PREP 5 MINS • COOK 1–1¼ HRS • CALS PER PORTION 140 • FAT PER PORTION 1 G

1 Preheat the oven to gas mark 6/200°C (400°F). Prick the potatoes well with a fork or a sharp knife and place on a baking tray with the garlic cloves. Bake for 1–1¼ hours until soft.
2 Scoop out the potato flesh and mix with the vegetable stock and warm milk. Squeeze the garlic cloves from their skin and mix the soft, roasted insides of the garlic into the potatoes. Mash together and season with salt and pepper.

3 large potatoes

9 garlic cloves, unpeeled

4 tablespoons vegetable stock

4 tablespoons warm skimmed milk

chips

SERVES 4 • PREP 10 MINS • COOK 30–40 MINS • CALS PER PORTION 180 • FAT PER PORTION 1.5 G

4 large baking potatoes, about 1 kg (2¼ lb) in weight

low-fat cooking spray

1 Preheat the oven to gas mark 7/220°C (425°F). Cut the baking potatoes into chips leaving on the skins. Spray the chips with low-fat cooking spray then spray a non-stick baking tray and spread out the chips on the tray.
2 Place the baking tray in the oven and bake for 20 minutes. Turn the chips and bake for another 10–20 minutes. Sprinkle with salt and serve.

LOW-FAT DESSERTS
apple crumble

SERVES 8 • PREP 15 MINS • COOK 40 MINS • CALS PER PORTION 220 • FAT PER PORTION 5 G

1 Preheat the oven to gas mark 7/220°C (425°F). Toss the chopped cooking apples in a bowl with the lemon juice. In another bowl combine the sugar, plain flour, lemon zest and spices. Sprinkle the mixture over the apples then put the apples in a 23 cm (9 in) pie dish.

2 To make the crumble mixture, mix together the soft brown sugar and the rolled oats, add the wholemeal flour and cinnamon, then rub in the margarine.

3 Spoon the crumble over the apple mixture and bake in the oven for 40 minutes.

700 g (1½ lb) peeled and chopped cooking apples

2 teaspoons lemon juice

50 g (2 oz) sugar

50 g (2 oz) plain flour

grated zest of 1 lemon

1 teaspoon ground cinnamon

1 teaspoon ground nutmeg

For the crumble:

3 tablespoons soft brown sugar

50 g (2 oz) rolled oats

50 g (2 oz) wholemeal flour

1 teaspoon ground cinnamon

15 g (½ oz) margarine

fruit salad with citrus greek yogurt

SERVES 10 • PREP 10 MINS PLUS STANDING • COOK NONE • CALS PER PORTION 100 • FAT PER PORTION 1 G

900 g (2 lb) strawberries, hulled

3 pawpaws, roughly chopped

7 kiwi fruits, peeled and sliced

1 stem lemon grass (optional)

450 ml (¾ pint) apple and mango juice

250 g (9 oz) low-fat Greek yogurt

grated zest of ½ lime

1 Halve the strawberries. Put all the fruit in a glass bowl, add the lemon grass, if using, and pour over the apple and mango juice. Cover and leave to infuse for 1 hour.
2 Mix the Greek yogurt with the lime zest, then serve the fruit topped with a generous dollop of the yogurt.

banana yogurt sundae

SERVES 4 • PREP 10 MINS, PLUS CHILLING • COOK NONE • CALS PER PORTION 170 • FAT PER PORTION 2 G

1 Divide the sliced bananas among four sundae dishes or large wine glasses.
2 Mix the sugar and spice gently into the yogurt – it doesn't matter if the yogurt is streaky.
3 Spoon the yogurt mixture on top of the fruit in each glass, then top with the crushed biscuits. Serve lightly chilled.

2 large or 4 small ripe bananas, sliced

4 teaspoons dark muscovado or soft brown sugar

2 pinches of freshly grated nutmeg, cinnamon or mixed spice

300 g (10 oz) low-fat bio yogurt

2 reduced-fat digestive biscuits, crushed

pears in hot chocolate

SERVES 5 • PREP 10 MINS • COOK 10 MINS • CALS PER PORTION 70 • FAT PER PORTION 0.5 G

410 g (approx 14 oz) can pear halves in natural juice, drained

cocoa powder, for dusting

For the custard sauce:

300 ml (½ pint) skimmed milk

2 teaspoons sugar

2 teaspoons custard powder

2 teaspoons cocoa powder

1 Make up the custard sauce with skimmed milk and sugar, according to the custard packet instructions, adding cocoa powder with the custard powder.

2 Pour the chocolate custard over the pears, dust with a little cocoa powder and serve immediately.

plum clafoutis

SERVES 4 • PREP 10 MINS, PLUS RESTING • COOK 45–50 MINS • CALS PER PORTION 315 • FAT PER PORTION 4 G

1 Preheat the oven to gas mark 4/180°C (350°C). Arrange the plums or other seasonal fruit in the bottom of a 1.1 litre (2 pint) ovenproof baking dish.
2 In a food processor or a large bowl, combine the eggs, egg whites, flour, buttermilk, vanilla extract, sugar and cinnamon. Whisk until well combined then leave to rest for 30 minutes.
3 Pour the rested batter over the plums and bake in the oven for 45–50 minutes until golden on top.

450 g (1 lb) plums, pitted and quartered, or other seasonal fruit, such as cherries or nectarines

For the batter:

2 eggs, plus 2 egg whites

150 g (5 oz) plain flour

268 ml (approx ½ pint) carton buttermilk

1 teaspoon vanilla extract

75 g (3 oz) caster sugar

¼ teaspoon ground cinnamon

ricotta and rhubarb pots

SERVES 4 • PREP 5 MINS • COOK 30 MINS • CALS PER PORTION 125 • FAT PER PORTION 5 G

250 g (9 oz) rhubarb, sliced into 2.5 cm (1 in) pieces

1 cm (½ in) piece of fresh root ginger, finely chopped

grated zest of 1 unwaxed lemon

50 g (2 oz) caster sugar

200 g (7 oz) tub ricotta

1 Preheat the oven to gas mark 5/190°C (375°F). In a heavy-based saucepan, place the rhubarb, ginger, lemon zest and sugar. Add 75 ml (3 fl oz) water, bring to the boil and simmer for 10 minutes until rhubarb is soft. Set aside to cool.

2 When the rhubarb mixture has cooled, blend with the ricotta in a large mixing bowl until well combined.

3 Pour the mixture into four 7.5 cm (3 in) ramekins and bake in the oven for 20 minutes until set. Remove and serve immediately.

Variation

For a more dramatic presentation, place a 7.5 cm (3 in) pastry cutter on top of each ramekin. Pour the rhubarb mixture halfway up the inside of the cutter and cook as above. Carefully remove and serve. (Besides being a low-fat soft cheese, ricotta sets like a mousse when cooked in the oven.)

mixed summer fruit trifle

SERVES 4 • PREP 10 MINS • COOK NONE • CALS PER PORTION 180 • FAT PER PORTION 3 G

1 In a large bowl, mix together the cassis, if using, and cranberry juice. Dip the sponge biscuit halves into the juice to soak up the liquid and arrange 2 halves at the bottom of each of four large glass tumblers.

2 Top the soaked sponge biscuits with mixed summer fruits and pour over the yogurt.

3 Decorate with a light dusting of cocoa powder. Chill then serve.

Tips

Cassis is a liqueur made from blackcurrants, which, mixed with champagne, becomes the drink, Kir Royale. Use fresh raspberries and blueberries, or choose your own selection of mixed berries. If you use frozen mixed summer fruits, available in most large supermarkets, defrost them first.

1 tablespoon cassis (optional)

75 ml (3 fl oz) cranberry juice

4 sponge biscuits, halved

150 g (5 oz) mixed fresh summer fruits

2 x 200 g (7 oz) tubs low-fat vanilla-flavoured yogurt

4 teaspoons cocoa powder

moroccan pudding

SERVES 4 • PREP 5 MINS • COOK 15 MINS • CALS PER PORTION 225 • FAT PER PORTION 1 G

1 Pour the milk into a large, heavy-based saucepan and add the sugar, orange zest, vanilla extract, cinnamon, couscous and a pinch of salt. Heat for 5 minutes, stirring continuously to prevent sticking.
2 Add the apricots and continue to cook for 5–10 minutes, until the pudding has thickened.
3 Chill and serve with slices of orange and low-fat Greek yogurt.

Tip
You can replace the vanilla extract with 1 vanilla pod. Remember to remove it before serving or, alternatively, use it to decorate the pudding.

900 ml (1½ pints) skimmed milk

2 tablespoons caster sugar

grated zest of 1 orange

1 teaspoon vanilla extract

½ teaspoon ground cinnamon

125 g (4 oz) couscous

125 g (4 oz) ready-to-eat dried apricots, roughly chopped

banana bread

SERVES 6 • PREP 15 MINS • COOK 45 MINS • CALS PER PORTION 183 • FAT PER PORTION 0.8 G

1 Preheat the oven to gas mark 2/150°C (300°F). Put the low-fat spread in a bowl. Add the mashed bananas, soft brown sugar, egg, vanilla extract and milk and blend until smooth.
2 Fold the self-raising flour, bicarbonate of soda, mixed spice and chopped dates into the mixture. Pour into a lightly oiled 450 g (1 lb) loaf tin and bake in the oven for 45 minutes.

25 g (1 oz) low-fat spread

3 bananas, mashed

1 tablespoon soft brown sugar

1 egg, beaten

½ teaspoon vanilla extract

3 tablespoons skimmed milk

150 g (5 oz) self-raising flour

¼ teaspoon bicarbonate of soda

½ teaspoon mixed spice

1 tablespoon chopped dates

banana and chocolate chip muffins

MAKES 10–12 • PREP 15 MINS • COOK 25 MINS • CALS PER MUFFIN 270–255 • FAT PER MUFFIN 4–3 G

2 bananas, chopped

1 tablespoon vegetable oil

1 egg, plus 2 egg whites

250 ml (8 fl oz) skimmed milk

400 g (14 oz) self-raising white flour

150 g (5 oz) caster sugar

½ teaspoon bicarbonate of soda

2 teaspoons finely grated orange zest

50 g (2 oz) dark chocolate, finely chopped

1 Preheat the oven to gas 5/190°C (375°F). Place the bananas in a food processor or blender with the vegetable oil, egg and egg whites and the skimmed milk. Work the ingredients to a purée.
2 Sift the self-raising flour, caster sugar and bicarbonate of soda into a large bowl. Stir in the orange zest and chopped dark chocolate. Fold in the banana mixture until just blended.
3 Place 10–12 paper muffin cases, measuring 6.5 cm (2½ in) in diameter, on a baking tray. Spoon the muffin mixture into the cases until two-thirds full. Bake in the oven for 25 minutes or until lightly brown and risen.

noodles, rice and pasta

There are many varieties of noodles, rice and pasta available (see pages 12–13). For successful pasta, cook in plenty of boiling, salted water and drain when the pasta is just tender. Rice should be measured by volume and the amount of water is double – remember to leave rice alone while it is cooking.

sweet and sour prawns with noodles

SERVES 4 • PREP 5 MINS • COOK 20 MINS • CALS PER PORTION 590 • FAT PER PORTION 15 G

1 Cook the noodles in a large saucepan of boiling water for about 4 minutes, drain and set aside.
2 Heat the oil in a large frying pan or wok, add the red peppers and stir-fry for 2 minutes. Add the prawns and cook for a further 2 minutes. Add the vinegar and cook for a further 1 minute.
3 Mix together the passata and the sugar and add to the pan. Cook for 5 minutes until the sauce is piping hot and slightly thickened. Remove from the heat, stir into the noodles with the coriander and chilli, if using, and serve.

350 g (12 oz) egg noodles

2 tablespoons vegetable oil

2 red peppers, cored, deseeded and cut into strips

450 g (1 lb) cooked peeled prawns, defrosted if frozen

2 tablespoons white wine vinegar

500 g (1 lb 2 oz) carton passata

2 tablespoons sugar

1 handful of chopped fresh coriander (optional)

1 green chilli, sliced (optional)

quick noodles with crab and coriander

SERVES 4 • PREP 20 MINS • COOK 20 MINS • CALS PER PORTION 240 • FAT PER PORTION 7 G

175 g (6 oz) rice noodles

1 tablespoon sesame or vegetable oil

1 garlic clove, crushed

6 shallots, sliced

1 red pepper, cored, deseeded and sliced

½ teaspoon finely grated fresh root ginger

240 g (approx 8½ oz) can crabmeat, drained and roughly flaked

1 tablespoon chopped fresh coriander

1 tablespoon teriyaki or soy sauce

1 Add the rice noodles to boiling water and soak, according to packet instructions.

2 Meanwhile, heat the oil in a wok or large frying pan until lightly smoking, then stir-fry the garlic, shallots and red pepper for 2–3 minutes.

3 Add the ginger, crabmeat, coriander and teriyaki or soy sauce and stir-fry for 2 minutes more. Season with salt and ground black pepper, then serve with the drained noodles.

garlic prawns with sesame noodles

SERVES 4 • PREP 5 MINS • COOK 5 MINS • CALS PER PORTION 580 • FAT PER PORTION 19 G

1 Cook the noodles according to packet instructions. Drain and sprinkle with sesame seeds and chopped coriander.
2 Meanwhile, heat a wok or large frying pan over a high heat until hot. Add the oil and, when slightly smoking, add the garlic. After 1 minute add the spring onions. Stir-fry for a further 1 minute or until golden brown.
3 Add the prawns and cook for 2 minutes more. Season with salt and ground black pepper and then serve immediately with the noodles.

375 g (13 oz) egg noodles

2 tablespoons sesame seeds

2 tablespoons roughly chopped fresh coriander

2 tablespoons olive oil

3 tablespoons finely sliced garlic

2 spring onions, thinly sliced

450 g (1 lb) raw peeled tiger prawns

bean curd and cashew stir-fry

SERVES 2 • PREP 10 MINS • COOK 5 MINS • CALS PER PORTION 300 • FAT PER PORTION 8 G

1 tablespoon oil

3 cm (1¼ in) piece of fresh root ginger, peeled and grated

1 garlic clove, crushed

100 g (3½ oz) bean curd, cut into squares

1 red pepper, cored, deseeded and cut into strips

1 yellow pepper, cored, deseeded and cut into strips

100 g (3½ oz) broccoli, cut into 5 cm (2 in) strips

100 g (3½ oz) mangetout, trimmed

4 spring onions, sliced

1 tablespoon crushed cashew nuts

1 tablespoon sherry

1 tablespoon rich soy sauce

400 g (14 oz) cooked egg noodles

1 Heat the oil in a heavy pan or wok until very hot. Toss in the ginger and garlic for 10 seconds. Add the squares of bean curd and fry for 1 minute. Remove the bean curd and set aside.

2 Add all the vegetables to the pan, together with the cashew nuts, and fry for 1–2 minutes.

3 Add the sherry and soy sauce. Return the bean curd to the pan. Stir carefully for a few seconds, then serve immediately with the cooked egg noodles.

pumpkin, thyme and feta pilaf

SERVES 4 • PREP 10–15 MINS • COOK 40 MINS • CALS PER PORTION 490 • FAT PER PORTION 22 G

1 Preheat the oven to gas mark 7/220°C (425°F). Place the diced pumpkin and onion wedges in a large roasting tin, stir in the olive oil and half the thyme. Add plenty of pepper and a little salt. Roast in the oven for 20 minutes or until the vegetables begin to colour.

2 Add the rice and the hot vegetable stock to the tin, stir well. Cover the roasting tin with foil and seal well around the edges. Return to the oven for 20 minutes.

3 Carefully remove the foil and gently stir through the rest of the thyme and the feta cheese to serve.

Tips

A serrated bread knife makes peeling the pumpkin easier. Add a few good-quality, pitted black olives to the recipe for extra flavour. This dish can be served alone but also makes an excellent accompaniment to grilled or roasted lamb.

700 g (1½ lb) pumpkin, peeled and with the flesh chopped into 2.5 cm (1 in) dice

1 large red onion, sliced into thin wedges

4 tablespoons olive oil

2 tablespoons chopped fresh thyme

250 g (9 oz) long-grain rice

750 ml (1¼ pints) hot vegetable stock

200 g (7 oz) feta cheese, crumbled

mascarpone risotto with pancetta

SERVES 4 • PREP 10 MINS • COOK 25 MINS • CALS PER PORTION 560 • FAT PER PORTION 31 G

3 tablespoons olive oil

1 onion, finely chopped

2 garlic cloves, crushed

250 g (9 oz) risotto rice

150 ml (¼ pint) dry white wine

750 ml (1¼ pints) hot vegetable stock

125 g (4 oz) pancetta or bacon pieces

50 g (2 oz) unsalted butter

50 g (2 oz) Parmesan, freshly grated

50 g (2 oz) mascarpone (optional)

50 g (2 oz) rocket (optional)

1 Heat 2 tablespoons oil in a heavy-based pan. Add the onion and garlic and cook for 5 minutes until softened.
2 Add the risotto rice and, stirring continuously, cook over a medium heat for 2–3 minutes. Add the dry white wine and keep stirring over a medium heat until evaporated.
3 Add one ladleful of hot stock and cook until absorbed. Continue adding the stock one ladleful at a time until all the stock has been absorbed and the rice is cooked – about 15–20 minutes.
4 Meanwhile, grill the pancetta or bacon for 5 minutes until golden. Add it to the risotto with the butter and the Parmesan. Stir in the mascarpone and rocket, if using. Sprinkle with lots of ground black pepper and serve.

lemon chicken risotto

SERVES 4 • PREP 25 MINS • COOK 25 MINS • CALS PER PORTION 400 • FAT PER PORTION 9 G

1 Place one-third of the chicken stock in a saucepan with the risotto rice and bring to the boil. Simmer until virtually all of the stock has been absorbed, then add half of the remaining stock, stirring occasionally.

2 Meanwhile, spray a non-stick frying pan with the cooking spray and fry the chicken for 4–5 minutes until browned. Set aside.

3 When the stock has been absorbed by the rice, add the lemon zest and juice. Add the remaining stock and the cooked chicken.

4 Continue cooking until almost all the stock has gone and the rice is cooked. Stir in the grated Parmesan, season with ground black pepper and serve.

1 chicken stock cube dissolved in 750 ml (1¼ pints) boiling water

250 g (9 oz) risotto rice

low-fat cooking spray

4 skinless, boneless chicken breasts, cubed

2 tablespoons grated zest and juice of 1 lemon

50 g (2 oz) Parmesan, freshly grated

turkey risotto

SERVES 2 • PREP 15 MINS • COOK 35 MINS • CALS PER PORTION 463 • FAT PER PORTION 9 G

1 teaspoon olive oil

1 small onion, chopped

1 garlic clove, crushed

125 g (4 oz) turkey breast, diced

150 g (5 oz) easy-cook brown rice

2 chicken stock cubes dissolved in 1 litre (1¾ pints) boiling water

1 small pinch of saffron strands, crushed

1 celery stick, sliced

1 small red pepper, cored, deseeded and chopped

75 g (3 oz) frozen peas

1 tablespoon low-fat crème fraîche

1 Heat the olive oil in a pan. Add the onion and garlic and fry lightly. Add the diced turkey breast and cook for 3 minutes.

2 Add the rice, chicken stock, saffron, celery and red pepper and bring to the boil. Simmer, uncovered, for about 15 minutes. Add more water if necessary.

3 Finally, add the peas and cook for a further 10 minutes. Stir in the crème fraîche, season with salt and black pepper and serve.

mother's own paella

SERVES 6 • PREP 15 MINS • COOK 40 MINS • CALS PER PORTION 370 • FAT PER PORTION 10 G

1 Heat the olive oil in a large, deep frying pan. Add the diced onion and crushed garlic. Cook over a low heat for 5 minutes until soft and translucent.
2 Add the chicken pieces and cook for 5 minutes on each side until lightly browned.
3 Add the rice, saffron and stock to the pan and mix well. Bring to the boil, reduce and simmer for 15 minutes, stirring occasionally to prevent the rice from sticking. Add more stock, if needed.
4 Add the white wine, mussels, prawns and squid and season with salt and ground black pepper. Cover the pan with a lid or foil, and cook for a further 8–10 minutes. Add the lemon juice, sprinkle over the parsley and serve with lemon wedges.

2 tablespoons olive oil

1 large onion, diced

2 garlic cloves, chopped then crushed

4 chicken pieces, skinned and cut into large chunks

200 g (7 oz) long-grain rice

large pinch of saffron strands, crushed

600 ml (1 pint) hot chicken stock

200 ml (7 fl oz) white wine

12 mussels, cleaned

8 large raw, unpeeled prawns

75 g (3 oz) squid, cleaned and cut into rings

juice of 1 lemon

1 small bunch of fresh flat leaf parsley, roughly chopped

1 lemon, cut into wedges, to serve

fishy stuffed tomatoes

SERVES 2 • PREP 10 MINS • COOK 15 MINS • CALS PER PORTION 560 • FAT PER PORTION 34 G

1 Hollow out the centre of the beef tomatoes.
2 Heat the olive oil in a pan. Add the red onion, garlic and red pepper and fry lightly. Add the flaked, peppered mackerel and the insides of the beef tomatoes. Cook for a further 3 minutes.
3 Combine the mackerel mixture with the hot, cooked rice and stir in plenty of freshly chopped basil. Use the rice mixture to stuff the hollowed-out tomatoes. Cook gently under a preheated grill for 5 minutes then serve.

2–3 large beef tomatoes

1 teaspoon olive oil

1 red onion, chopped

1 garlic clove, crushed

1 red pepper, cored, deseeded and diced

2 fillets vacuum-packed peppered mackerel, flaked

175 g (6 oz) hot, cooked rice

1 handful of fresh basil, chopped

avocado, rice and kidney bean salad

SERVES 6 • PREP 20 MINS • COOK 35 MINS • CALS PER PORTION 577 • FAT PER PORTION 24 G

1 Cook the rice in a pan of boiling, salted water according to packet instructions then set aside to cool.
2 Meanwhile, toast the pinenuts to bring out their nutty flavour. Spread them on a baking tray and place under a preheated grill for a few minutes. Keep checking and shaking the tray so that the pinenuts cook fairly evenly and do not burn. Leave to cool.
3 In a large bowl, gently mix together the avocados, lemon juice, kidney beans, green chilli and spring onions.
4 Add the avocado mixture to the cold rice and stir in the toasted pinenuts and coriander. Drizzle with olive oil and add the lemon zest. Season to taste with salt and ground black pepper and give it one last stir. Chill until required.

Variation

Bulgar wheat can be used instead of brown rice. Simply cover it with boiling hot water, drizzle a little olive oil over and cover for 20 minutes. Fluff up with a fork and leave to cool.

500 g (1 lb 2 oz) brown rice

75 g (3 oz) pinenuts

2 ripe avocados, peeled, stoned and sliced

grated zest and juice of 1 lemon

410 g (approx 14 oz) can red kidney beans, drained and rinsed

1 large green chilli, deseeded and finely sliced

1 bunch of spring onions, sliced

1 large bunch of fresh coriander, chopped

2 tablespoons olive oil

herby tuna salad

SERVES 2 • PREP 5 MINS • COOK 5 MINS • CALS PER PORTION 470 • FAT PER PORTION 7 G

1 Heat the olive oil in a pan. Meanwhile, core, deseed and dice the red pepper. Add the onion, pepper and mushrooms to the pan and fry lightly.
2 Add the vegetables to the cooked rice. Drain the tuna and stir it in with plenty of freshly chopped coriander. Season with salt and ground black pepper and serve.

1 teaspoon olive oil

1 red onion, chopped

1 red pepper

125 g (4 oz) chopped mushrooms

175 g (6 oz) cooked brown rice

100 g (3½ oz) can tuna in brine

1 handful of fresh coriander

warm summer rice salad

SERVES 6 • PREP 15 MINS • COOK 25 MINS • CALS PER PORTION 390 • FAT PER PORTION 12 G

375 g (13 oz) long-grain rice

175 g (6 oz) fresh or frozen peas

2 yellow peppers, cored, deseeded and diced

3 tomatoes, roughly chopped

4 tablespoons grated Parmesan

2 tablespoons roughly chopped fresh flat leaf parsley

For the dressing:

1 tablespoon mustard

1 tablespoon red wine vinegar

4 tablespoons olive oil

1 Cook the rice in a saucepan of boiling, salted water according to packet instructions. Just before it is cooked, add the peas and cook for 1 minute. Drain then return the rice and peas to the pan.
2 To make the dressing, mix together the mustard and vinegar. Whisk in the olive oil and season with salt and black pepper.
3 Stir the dressing into the hot rice and peas mixture. Add the rest of the ingredients and mix gently. Serve warm or cold.

chinese lamb stir-fry

SERVES 1 • PREP 20 MINS • COOK 20 MINS • CALS PER PORTION 525
FAT PER PORTION 19 G

1 Cook the spaghetti in a large saucepan of boiling, salted water according to packet instructions. Drain, rinse in cold water and set aside.
2 Heat a heavy-based wok or frying pan until quite hot, then dry-fry the strips of lamb for about 2 minutes until browned. Remove and keep warm.
3 Add the sunflower oil to the pan and heat until quite hot. Add the vegetables and stir-fry for about 2 minutes until just softened. Return the lamb to the pan.
4 Mix in the sherry or vermouth, if using, the soy sauce and sesame oil. Heat well until bubbling, then stir in the cooked spaghetti and season with salt and ground black pepper. Reheat, then sprinkle over the sesame seeds and serve.

50 g (2 oz) quick-cooking dried spaghetti

100 g (3½ oz) boneless leg lamb steak, trimmed of fat and cut into strips

1 teaspoon sunflower oil

¼ small red pepper, cored, deseeded and thinly sliced

2 spring onions, sliced

1 carrot, cut into thin sticks

1 small courgette, cut into thin sticks

1 tablespoon dry sherry or vermouth (optional)

2 tablespoons light soy sauce

1 teaspoon sesame oil

1 teaspoon sesame seeds

bacon and tomato pasta bake

SERVES 4 • PREP 15 MINS • COOK 20 MINS • CALS PER PORTION 820 • FAT PER PORTION 47 G

1 Preheat the oven to gas mark 6/200°C (400°F). Cook the pasta in a large saucepan of boiling, salted water according to packet instructions. Drain well.

2 Meanwhile, fry the bacon in a frying pan for 5 minutes until cooked and brown. Remove and set aside.

3 In a large bowl combine the cooked pasta and bacon with the sun-dried tomatoes and four-cheese sauce. Pour into an ovenproof dish, sprinkle over the breadcrumbs and cheese then cook for 20 minutes until golden.

4 Sprinkle over the chopped parsley and lemon zest to garnish, and serve immediately.

300 g (11 oz) dried penne

200 g (7 oz) bacon pieces

200 g (7 oz) jar sun-dried tomatoes, drained and roughly chopped

350 g (12 oz) jar four-cheese pasta sauce

25 g (1 oz) white breadcrumbs

50 g (2 oz) Parmesan or cheddar, freshly grated

2 tablespoons roughly chopped fresh parsley

grated zest of 1 lemon

creamy ham and cheese pasta

SERVES 4 • PREP 15 MINS • COOK 15 MINS • CALS PER PORTION 340 • FAT PER PORTION 6 G

1 Cook the pasta in a large saucepan of boiling, salted water according to packet instructions, until tender yet firm.

2 Meanwhile, gently heat the cheese and milk in a large saucepan until smooth. When just about to boil, stir in the strips of ham. Remove the pan from the heat and set aside.

3 Drain the pasta thoroughly, then return to its pan. Add the cheese sauce and toss to coat thoroughly. Season to taste with salt and ground black pepper and serve immediately.

225 g (8 oz) dried tagliatelle

225 g (8 oz) low-fat soft cheese with garlic and herbs

5 tablespoons skimmed milk

50 g (2 oz) lean ham, cut into strips

pasta, bacon and artichoke salad

SERVES 6 • PREP 20 MINS • COOK 15 MINS • CALS PER PORTION 580 • FAT PER PORTION 27 G

500 g (1 lb 2 oz) dried penne

1 tablespoon olive oil

130 g (approx 4 oz) packet cubed pancetta or 12 rashers streaky bacon, chopped

2 x 400 g (14 oz) cans artichoke hearts, drained and halved

350 g (12 oz) jar pitted green olives in brine, drained

6 tablespoons mayonnaise

1 bunch of fresh flat leaf parsley, chopped

1 Cook the pasta in a large saucepan of boiling, salted water according to packet instructions. Drain, rinse thoroughly in cold water and set aside to cool.

2 Meanwhile, heat the oil in a small frying pan and fry the pancetta or bacon for about 2–3 minutes until crispy. Leave to drain on absorbent kitchen paper.

3 When the pasta is cold, add the artichokes, olives and pancetta or bacon and stir well. Mix in the mayonnaise and stir to coat the pasta. Stir in the chopped parsley and season well with salt and ground black pepper. Chill until required.

pasta with classic tomato sauce

SERVES 4 • PREP 5 MINS • COOK 30 MINUTES • CALS PER PORTION 650 • FAT PER PORTION 24 G

1 Heat 3 tablespoons olive oil in a saucepan. Add the chopped onions and crushed garlic and cook for 4 minutes over a medium heat until soft and translucent.
2 Add the passata and dried mixed herbs and season with salt and black pepper. Simmer for 25 minutes, stirring occasionally.
3 Meanwhile, cook the pasta in a large saucepan of boiling, salted water according to packet instructions. Drain and toss with the remaining 1 tablespoon olive oil. Add the sauce to the pasta and stir through. Sprinkle with Parmesan and basil leaves, drizzle with olive oil and serve.

4 tablespoons olive oil, plus extra for drizzling

2 onions, chopped

2 garlic cloves, chopped then crushed

2 x 500 g (1 lb 2 oz) cartons passata

2 teaspoons dried mixed herbs

450 g (1 lb) dried spaghetti

75 g (3 oz) Parmesan, freshly grated

1 handful of fresh basil leaves, to garnish

Tip
The sauce may be frozen for up to three months. Defrost thoroughly before using.

pasta with fennel and crème fraîche

SERVES 6 • PREP 10 MINS • COOK 10–15 MINS • CALS PER PORTION 560 • FAT PER PORTION 15 G

1 Bring a large saucepan of water to the boil. Add the fennel and boil for 1 minute then remove with a slotted spoon. Toss with the olive oil and cook under a preheated grill until lightly charred – about 4 minutes.

2 Meanwhile, add the pasta to the boiling water and cook according to packet instructions. Drain the pasta and return to the warm saucepan.

3 Stir in the crème fraîche, almonds, parsley, lemon juice and grilled fennel. Season with salt and black pepper and serve hot.

2 large fennel bulbs, sliced

2 tablespoons olive oil

700 g (1½ lb) dried pasta shapes

200 ml (7 fl oz) tub crème fraîche

50 g (2 oz) flaked almonds, toasted

2 tablespoons roughly chopped fresh flat leaf parsley

juice of ½ lemon

spaghetti with red pesto and olives

SERVES 4 • PREP 5 MINS • COOK 10–12 MINS • CALS PER PORTION 630 • FAT PER PORTION 18 G

1 In a large heavy-based saucepan, mix together the canned tomatoes, red pesto and olives. Bring to the boil then simmer gently for 10 minutes, until thickened. Season with salt and ground black pepper.

2 Meanwhile, cook the spaghetti in a large pan of boiling, salted water according to packet instructions.

3 Drain the spaghetti. Pour the sauce over the spaghetti to coat. Serve in pasta bowls and garnish with fresh coriander.

400 g (14 oz) can chopped tomatoes with garlic

190 g (approx 7 oz) jar red pesto

125 g (4 oz) pitted olives, halved

400 g (14 oz) dried spaghetti

2 tablespoons roughly chopped fresh coriander

monkfish parcels

SERVES 2 • PREP 20 MINS • COOK 20 MINS • CALS PER PORTION 460 • FAT PER PORTION 10 G

16 large spinach leaves

2 tablespoons white wine

1 tablespoon lemon juice

2 shallots, chopped

2 x 175 g (6 oz) monkfish fillets

150 g (5 oz) dried tagliatelle

2–3 tablespoons vinaigrette

1 Blanch the spinach leaves in a large saucepan of boiling water. Drain, run under cold water then pat dry.

2 In a small saucepan cook together the white wine, lemon juice and shallots for 3–4 minutes. Allow to cool.

3 Arrange 8 spinach leaves on a chopping board so that they overlap. Spread over 1 tablespoon of the shallot mix. Place a monkfish fillet on top in the centre and wrap up the leaves to enclose. Repeat with the other fillet.

4 Place the wrapped parcels on a heatproof plate and steam for 12–15 minutes.

5 Meanwhile, cook the pasta in a large saucepan of boiling, salted water according to packet instructions. Drain well and serve with the monkfish, accompanied by the vinaigrette.

quick creamy prawn pasta

SERVES 4 • PREP 5 MINS • COOK 5 MINS • CALS PER PORTION 465 • FAT PER PORTION 18 G

1 Cook the pasta in a large saucepan of boiling, salted water according to packet instructions.
2 Meanwhile, heat a large frying pan and spray with the low-fat cooking spray. Add the garlic and fry until just turning golden. Add the prawns, vinegar or sherry and season with salt and ground black pepper. Stir-fry for 4 minutes, or until the prawns are heated through.
3 Remove the pan from the heat then stir in the crème fraîche and fresh parsley.
4 Drain the cooked pasta, toss with the creamy sauce and season to taste. Serve immediately.

350 g (12 oz) dried penne pasta

low-fat cooking spray

4 garlic cloves, chopped

200 g (7 oz) cooked peeled prawns, defrosted if frozen

4 tablespoons sherry vinegar or dry sherry

150 ml (¼ pint) half-fat crème fraîche

1 small bunch of fresh parsley, chopped

tagliatelle with smoked salmon

SERVES 4 • PREP 25 MINS • COOK 25 MINS • CALS PER PORTION 355 • FAT PER PORTION 6 G

125 g (4 oz) low-fat soft cheese

175 g (6 oz) smoked salmon trimmings

4 tablespoons dry white wine

1 teaspoon lemon juice

1 tablespoon chopped fresh dill

350 g (12 oz) mangetout and tiny broccoli florets, mixed

225 g (8 oz) fresh tagliatelle or linguine

sprigs of fresh dill, to garnish

1 Put the soft cheese, 50 g (2 oz) of the smoked salmon trimmings, the white wine and the lemon juice into a blender or liquidizer and process until smooth.

2 Transfer the blended mixture to a small saucepan and heat through very gently. Do not allow the sauce to boil. Season with salt and ground black pepper, stir in the chopped dill and the remaining salmon trimmings.

3 Cook the mangetout and broccoli in a large saucepan of boiling, salted water for 5 minutes until just tender. Remove from the water with a slotted spoon, drain and set aside. Add the pasta to the boiling water for 2–3 minutes until just cooked. Drain thoroughly, then return the pasta to the warm saucepan.

4 Add the smoked salmon sauce, mangetout and broccoli to the cooked pasta, carefully folding them together. Serve immediately and garnish with sprigs of fresh dill.

meat and poultry

Always buy the best quality meat and poultry you can afford;
with careful planning you can get more for your money by
serving leftovers and making stock for soups. For roasts,
cook meat on a high heat first, then lower the temperature.
Let meat rest for 15 minutes after cooking to set the juices.

beef stew with cassis and orange

SERVES 4 • PREP 15 MINS • COOK 1 HR 40 MINS • CALS PER PORTION 470 • FAT PER PORTION 21 G

1 Heat half of the oil in a flameproof casserole and brown the beef in batches; remove the beef from the pan. Add the remaining oil, the onion and rosemary. Stir and cook gently for 5 minutes. Increase the heat and pour in the crème de cassis. Boil until reduced by half.
2 Return the browned beef to the pan and add the stock and orange juice. Bring to the boil then simmer, covered, for 1 hour. Add the carrots and cook for 30 minutes, by which time the meat should be tender, the sauce thickened and the carrots cooked.
3 Remove the sprigs of rosemary, stir in the mushrooms and orange zest and season with salt and ground black pepper. Cook for 5 minutes. If desired, serve with a pile of fluffy mashed potatoes to make a hearty winter meal.

4 tablespoons olive oil

750 g (1 lb 10 oz) stewing steak, cut into 4.5 cm (1¾ in) pieces

1 onion, finely chopped

3 sprigs of fresh rosemary

200 ml (7 fl oz) crème de cassis

450 ml (¾ pint) beef stock

grated zest and juice of 2 oranges

2 carrots, cut into 2.5 cm (1 in) pieces

450 g (1 lb) mixed mushrooms

steak and kidney pie

SERVES 4 • PREP 25 MINS • COOK 2 HRS 20 MINS • CALS PER PORTION 680 • FAT PER PORTION 36 G

1 tablespoon olive oil

2 large onions, finely chopped

700 g (1½ lb) chuck/braising steak, cut into 2.5 cm (1 in) cubes

175 g (6 oz) kidney, cut into 1 cm (½ in) cubes

225 g (8 oz) chestnut mushrooms, sliced

½ tablespoon plain flour

1 beef stock cube and 1 teaspoon meat extract, such as Bovril, dissolved in 450 ml (¾ pint) boiling water

½ teaspoon dried mixed herbs

½ teaspoon Worcestershire sauce

375 g (13 oz) packet puff pastry

1 tablespoon caraway seeds

1 egg, beaten

1 In a large saucepan, heat the oil and cook the onions for 2 minutes. Add the steak and kidney and cook for 5 minutes until brown on all sides. Add the mushrooms and cook for a further 5 minutes. Season with salt and ground black pepper.
2 Stir in the plain flour then gradually stir in the beef stock. Add the dried herbs and Worcestershire sauce. Bring to the boil, cover and simmer for 1–1½ hours, or until tender.
3 Preheat the oven to gas mark 3/160°C (325°F). Put the steak and kidney mixture in a heatproof pie dish. Roll out the pastry on a floured surface and sprinkle with the caraway seeds. Gently roll the pastry once to press in the seeds.
4 Dampen the edges of the pie dish with water. Cut narrow strips of pastry and lay them around the top edge of the dish. Dampen them with water then top with a lid of pastry. Pinch the edges of pastry together to seal, then trim.
5 Brush the pastry with beaten egg and sprinkle with salt. Bake in the oven for 30–35 minutes until the pastry is cooked and golden. Serve with green vegetables.

yankee pot roast

SERVES 6 • PREP 15 MINS • COOK 3 HRS–3 HRS 20 MINS • CALS PER PORTION 480 • FAT PER PORTION 20 G

1 Heat the oil in a flameproof casserole, add the garlic, carrots, celery and onion and cook for 6–8 minutes until soft. Add the wine and simmer for 5 minutes until reduced by half.

2 Add the beef joint, beef stock, bay leaves and bouquet garni to the casserole. If the beef is not submerged, top up the pan with water. Bring to the boil, cover and simmer for 2½–3 hours, turning the beef every 30 minutes. Skim the surface to remove any scum.

3 Remove the beef, wrap it in foil and set aside. Strain off the vegetables and herbs and discard them. Return the liquid to the casserole. Skim off any excess fat and boil the stock until reduced to about 600 ml (1 pint).

4 Melt the butter in a small pan, add the flour and cook for 1–2 minutes, stirring continuously. Remove the pan from the heat and gradually add the reduced cooking liquid, stirring until smooth. Return the pan to the heat and cook for 3–4 minutes more, until thickened, then season with salt and black pepper.

5 Slice the beef and serve it with the sauce poured over the top. If desired, accompany the beef with mash and roasted carrots and cauliflower.

2 tablespoons vegetable oil

3 garlic cloves, chopped

2 carrots, peeled and roughly chopped

2 celery sticks, chopped

1 onion, roughly chopped

600 ml (1 pint) red wine

1.4 kg (3 lb) beef topside

900 ml (1½ pints) beef stock

2 bay leaves

1 bouquet garni

25 g (1 oz) butter

1 tablespoon flour

2 tablespoons olive oil

1 onion, finely chopped

2 garlic cloves, finely chopped

500 g (1 lb 2 oz) minced beef

300 ml (½ pint) red wine

400 g (14 oz) can chopped tomatoes

400 g (14 oz) can kidney beans in chilli sauce

600 g (1 lb 5 oz) sweet potatoes, peeled and cut into large chunks

600 g (1 lb 5 oz) potatoes, peeled and cut into large chunks

25 g (1 oz) butter

50 ml (2 fl oz) milk

spicy cottage pie

SERVES 4–6 • PREP 1 HR 5 MINS • COOK 30 MINS •
CALS PER PORTION 720–485 • FAT PER PORTION 24–16 G

1 Heat the oil in a large frying pan and cook the onion and garlic for 5 minutes. Add the mince, stir to break it up and cook over a high heat for 5 minutes until the mince is well browned.
2 Add the red wine and simmer for 2 minutes. Add the canned tomatoes and cook for 20 minutes. Add the kidney beans to the mixture and cook for a further 30 minutes.
3 Meanwhile, cook the sweet potatoes and potatoes in a large saucepan of boiling water for 20 minutes until cooked. Drain, return to the pan and place over the heat for 2 minutes to remove the excess water. Add the butter and milk and mash well.
4 Preheat the oven to gas mark 5/190°C (375°F). Put the meat in an ovenproof dish, top with mash and bake in the oven for 30 minutes.

classic beef casserole

SERVES 4 • PREP 45 MINS • COOK 3 HRS • CALS PER PORTION 600 • FAT PER PORTION 23 G

1 Preheat the oven to gas mark 3/160°C (325°F). In a large frying pan, heat 2 tablespoons of the oil and brown the beef in batches over a high heat. Remove the beef and set aside.

2 Fry the bacon for 5–10 minutes until browned. Remove and set aside on kitchen paper to drain. Add the remaining oil and sauté the shallots for 5 minutes or until cooked.

3 Transfer the bacon, beef and shallots to a heavy-based casserole. Pour 2 tablespoons water into the frying pan and, using a wooden spoon, loosen the sediment from the bottom. Add these juices to the casserole. Pour over the red wine, cover the casserole with a lid and cook in the oven for 1 hour.

4 Reduce the oven temperature to gas mark 2/150°C (300°F). Remove the casserole and add the carrots, celery, tomatoes, garlic, bay leaves, thyme and orange zest. Pour in enough water to cover, replace the lid and return the casserole to the oven for a further 2 hours until the meat is cooked and tender.

5 When the casserole is cooked, use a slotted spoon to remove the bay leaves and sprigs of thyme. For a tasty twist, stir in the tapenade and season with salt, black pepper and chopped parsley.

3 tablespoons olive oil

900 g (2 lb) braising steak, diced, fat and gristle removed

125 g (4 oz) unsmoked bacon, rinded and finely chopped

350 g (12 oz) shallots, peeled and trimmed

600 ml (1 pint) red wine

450 g (1 lb) carrots, peeled and thickly sliced

2 celery sticks, sliced

6 tomatoes, roughly chopped

2 garlic cloves, finely chopped

2 bay leaves

3 sprigs of fresh thyme

grated zest of 1 small orange

2 tablespoons tapenade

2 tablespoons roughly chopped fresh flat leaf parsley

Tips
Make the casserole a day ahead, as the flavour improves – it also freezes well, so you can make double the quantity and freeze half for another day.

warm beef sausage salad

SERVES 4 • PREP 5 MINS • COOK 30 MINS • CALS PER PORTION 668 • FAT PER PORTION 55 G

500 g (1 lb 2 oz) baby new potatoes, halved

8 beef sausages

150 ml (¼ pint) bottle fresh mustard and honey dressing

225 g (8 oz) cherry tomatoes

2 x 150 g (5 oz) packets endive and radicchio salad

1 Cook the potatoes in a large saucepan of boiling, salted water for 15 minutes until tender. Drain and set aside.

2 Meanwhile, place the sausages under a preheated hot grill for 20 minutes, turning occasionally until cooked. Slice each sausage into thirds on the diagonal.

3 In a heavy-based frying pan, mix together the mustard dressing with 2 tablespoons water. Add the sausages, potatoes and cherry tomatoes. Stir to coat in the dressing. Continue to heat until the cherry tomatoes burst and the dressing has reduced. Remove from the heat, toss in the salad leaves, mix and serve.

grilled steak with salsa verde

SERVES 4 • PREP 5 MINS • COOK 4–12 MINS • CALS PER PORTION 570 • FAT PER PORTION 43 G

1 Rub the steaks well with the oil, season with ground black pepper and cook under a preheated grill, as close to the heat as possible, turning the steaks every 2 minutes. Allow 3 minutes for rare; 5 minutes for medium and 8 minutes for well done.
2 To make the salsa verde, whizz the capers, garlic, mustard, parsley and olive oil together in a food processor or blender until smooth. Serve the sauce with the steak.

Variation
Traditionally served with red meat, this classic green sauce also works very well with grilled chicken or turkey.

4 x 225 g (8 oz) sirloin steaks

2 tablespoons vegetable oil

For the salsa verde:

2 tablespoons capers

2 garlic cloves, peeled and roughly chopped

1 tablespoon Dijon mustard

1 large bunch of fresh flat leaf parsley

150 ml (¼ pint) olive oil

lamb and mint kebabs with feta cheese salad

MAKES 6 KEBABS • PREP 30 MINS, PLUS 30 MINS SOAKING • COOK 8–20 MINS • CALS PER PORTION 490 • FAT PER PORTION 28 G

700 g (1½ lb) boneless leg of lamb, trimmed and cut into 18 x 5 cm (2 in) cubes

1 large red onion, cut into 12 wedges

3 firm tomatoes, cut into quarters

3 tablespoons olive oil

For the feta cheese salad:

125 ml (4 fl oz) olive oil

juice of 1 large lemon

1 teaspoon dried oregano

125 g (4 oz) pitted black olives, roughly chopped

200 g (7 oz) feta cheese, crumbled

3 tablespoons roughly chopped fresh mint

1 If you are using wooden skewers, soak them in cold water for 30 minutes before using.

2 Alternately thread 3 lamb pieces, 2 onion wedges and 2 tomato quarters on to each of six skewers. Brush with oil, season with salt and ground black pepper and set aside.

3 To make the feta cheese salad, mix the oil and lemon juice in a large bowl. Stir in the oregano, olives, feta and mint. Refrigerate until required.

4 Barbecue the kebabs over a medium heat for 8–10 minutes for rare, 13–15 minutes for medium or 18–20 minutes for well done, turning once. Alternatively, cook them under a preheated grill. Serve with the salad.

lamb with prunes and cinnamon

SERVES 4 • PREP 10 MINS • COOK 2¼ HRS • CALS PER PORTION 460 • FAT PER PORTION 18 G

1 Preheat the oven to gas mark 2/150°C (300°F). Season the lamb with salt and ground black pepper. Heat the oil in a large flameproof casserole and fry the lamb until it colours slightly. Add the onion rings and garlic and stir until softened.
2 Add all the other ingredients except the almonds and pour in a little water so everything is covered.
3 Cover the casserole and cook in the oven for up to 2 hours until the meat is tender and excess juices have evaporated.
4 Remove the cinnamon stick before serving and top with toasted almonds. Serve with couscous and chopped, fresh mint for a spicy supper with a twist.

400 g (14 oz) casserole lamb

1 tablespoon vegetable oil

1 large onion, sliced into rings

3 garlic cloves, chopped

12 prunes, soaked

450 g (1 lb) plum tomatoes

300 ml (½ pint) red wine

1 cinnamon stick

½ teaspoon freshly grated nutmeg

50 g (2 oz) toasted almonds

moussaka

SERVES 6 • PREP 25–30 MINS • COOK 1½ HRS • CALS PER PORTION 430• FAT PER PORTION 28 G

4 tablespoons sunflower oil

1 large onion, chopped

450 g (1 lb) minced lamb

400 g (14 oz) can chopped tomatoes

2 tablespoons roughly chopped fresh flat leaf parsley

¼ teaspoon ground cinnamon

900 g (2 lb) aubergines, trimmed and sliced

For the topping:

50 g (2 oz) butter

50 g (2 oz) plain white flour

600 ml (1 pint) milk

25 g (1 oz) Parmesan, freshly grated

1 egg yolk

2 tablespoons fresh breadcrumbs

1 Preheat the oven to gas mark 4/180°C (350°F). Heat 1 tablespoon of the oil in a large frying pan, add the onion and cook over a low heat for 10 minutes. Add the minced lamb and cook for a further 10 minutes until evenly browned. Add the tomatoes, parsley and cinnamon, and season well with salt and ground black pepper. Bring to the boil, cover and cook for 20 minutes.
2 Meanwhile, brush the aubergines with the rest of the oil and grill until soft and golden on both sides. Leave to drain.
3 To make the topping, melt the butter in a saucepan, stir in the flour and cook, stirring for 1 minute. Remove from the heat and slowly whisk in the milk. Return to the heat and bring to the boil, stirring for 3–4 minutes, until thickened. Cool slightly, beat in half the cheese and the egg yolk. Season with salt and pepper.
4 Arrange half the aubergines over the base of a 2.8 litre (5 pint) shallow ovenproof dish. Spread the meat on top and cover with the rest of the aubergines. Spoon the sauce over the top and sprinkle with the breadcrumbs and remaining cheese. Bake in the oven for 45 minutes, until golden.

leg of lamb with garlic, coriander and orange

SERVES 4 • PREP 10 MINS, PLUS MARINATING • COOK 1½ HRS, PLUS RESTING •
CALS PER PORTION 250 (WITH BONE), 400 (BONELESS) • FAT PER PORTION 13 G (WITH BONE), 22 G (BONELESS)

1 Rinse the lamb and pat it dry. Lift it into a shallow non-metallic dish. Make random slits all over the top of the lamb and insert about ½ teaspoon coriander seeds into each slit. Wrap a small strip of orange peel around each slice of garlic and insert in each slit.

2 Arrange the orange slices over the lamb, then cover and leave to marinate for at least 2 hours, or overnight.

3 Preheat the oven to gas mark 6/200°C (400°F). Lift the lamb into a roasting tin and cook for 1 hour. Brush the top with honey and return it to the oven for 30 minutes. Allow to stand for 15 minutes before carving. If desired, serve with courgettes, cabbage, carrots and roast potatoes.

half a leg of lamb, about 1 kg (2¼ lb) in weight

1 tablespoon coriander seeds, crushed

peel of 1 orange, plus 1 orange cut into slices

4 garlic cloves, sliced

1 tablespoon clear honey

lemon and sage pork

SERVES 4 • PREP 15 MINS, PLUS MARINATING • COOK 20 MINS • CALS PER PORTION 530 • FAT PER PORTION 40 G

150 ml (¼ pint) olive oil

50 ml (2 fl oz) white wine vinegar

3 lemons

2 tablespoons roughly chopped
fresh sage

1 garlic clove, crushed

4 pork loin steaks

1 tablespoon cumin seeds

1 Savoy cabbage, finely shredded

1 In a bowl, mix 125 ml (4 fl oz) of the olive oil with the white wine vinegar, juice and zest of 2 of the lemons, the sage and garlic. Season generously with salt and ground black pepper.
2 Arrange the pork in a shallow dish, pour over the marinade mixture to coat. Cut the remaining lemon into quarters and place on top of the pork. Cover and chill for at least 1 hour.
3 Preheat the oven to gas mark 4/180°C (350°F). Place the pork steaks in a roasting tin, pour over the remaining marinade and roast in the oven for 20 minutes.
4 Meanwhile, in a large frying pan, heat the remaining oil and fry the cumin seeds over a medium heat for 1 minute. Add the cabbage and sauté until tender. Serve with the pork and drizzle over the roasting juices.

Variation
Replace the pork with chicken breasts if preferred.

grilled pork chops with apple, fennel and onion

SERVES 4 • PREP 15 MINS, PLUS MARINATING • COOK 20 MINS • CALS PER PORTION 430 • FAT PER PORTION 26 G

1 In a shallow dish mix the crushed garlic with the lemon juice and 3 tablespoons of the olive oil. Add the pork chops, stir well, cover and leave to marinate for 30 minutes.

2 Heat the remaining oil in a large frying pan, add the sliced onions and gently fry for 5 minutes. Add the sliced fennel and cook for a further 5 minutes.

3 Remove the chops from the marinade and place them under a preheated grill on its highest setting. Cook for 5–6 minutes each side. Reserve the marinade.

4 Add the apple slices and fennel seeds to the onion mixture. Increase the heat and cook for 1 minute. Add the sugar and cook for 5 minutes until lightly caramelized. Add reserved marinade and cook for 1 minute, or until bubbling. Season with salt and pepper.

5 Serve the chops with the apple, fennel and onion mixture, accompanied by lemon wedges.

2 garlic cloves, crushed

2 tablespoons fresh lemon juice

5 tablespoons olive oil

4 pork chops

2 small onions, finely sliced

2 small fennel bulbs, finely sliced

2 Cox's Orange Pippin apples, cored and finely sliced

2 teaspoons fennel seeds

1 tablespoon caster sugar

lemon wedges, to serve

dolcelatte-stuffed pork chops
with roasted vegetables

SERVES 4 • PREP 30 MINS • COOK 50 MINS • CALS PER PORTION 450 • FAT PER PORTION 20 G

1 Preheat the oven to gas mark 6/200°C (400°F). Put the oil in a roasting tin and heat in the oven for 5 minutes. Add the parsnips, pears and onions to the tin, coat them in the oil and cook for about 30–35 minutes, until golden.

2 Combine the cheese and thyme. Cut the rind off the pork chops, make a slit through the fatty end and continue cutting through the flesh as deep as you can to form a pocket. Stuff the pockets with the cheese and thyme mixture and secure each with a cocktail stick to stop it oozing out.

3 Place the pork chops under a preheated grill on its highest setting. Grill the chops for 8–10 minutes on each side until browned. Season with ground black pepper and serve with roasted vegetables.

2 tablespoons olive oil

2 large parsnips, peeled and quartered

3 firm Conference pears, peeled, cored and quartered

3 small red onions, quartered

75 g (3 oz) Dolcelatte or Gorgonzola

4 sprigs of fresh thyme, stripped into leaves

4 large pork loin chops

pork sausage casserole

SERVES 4 • PREP 5 MINS • COOK 1¾ HRS • CALS PER PORTION 570 • FAT PER PORTION 39 G

1 Heat the olive oil in a large, heavy-based saucepan and gently fry the sausages for 10 minutes until brown. Cut the sausages in half diagonally if liked. Add the onion wedges and continue to fry for 3–4 minutes until soft.

2 Pour in the brown ale then stir in the Worcestershire sauce and mustard. Add the thyme, bring to the boil, then cover and simmer for 45 minutes.

3 Add the baby potatoes to the saucepan, cover and simmer for a further 45 minutes, until thickened. Season generously with salt and ground black pepper and serve.

1 tablespoon olive oil

8 good-quality pork sausages

1 small onion, cut into wedges

550 ml (approx 1 pint) bottle brown ale

1 tablespoon Worcestershire sauce

1 teaspoon ready-made English mustard

4 sprigs of fresh thyme

350 g (12 oz) baby potatoes, halved

pork, red lentil and dumpling soup

SERVES 4 • PREP 25 MINS • COOK 45 MINS • CALS PER PORTION 585 • FAT PER PORTION 29 G

3 tablespoons olive oil

1 onion, finely chopped

2 garlic cloves, crushed

1 sprig of fresh thyme

450 g (1 lb) loin pork steaks, cut into small chunks

2 fresh tomatoes, peeled and chopped

225 g (8 oz) red lentils, cooked

1 tablespoon tomato purée

1.1 litres (2 pints) vegetable stock

1 sweet potato, peeled and cut into 2.5 cm (1 in) cubes

1 tablespoon chopped fresh parsley

For the dumplings:

125 g (4 oz) plain flour

1 teaspoon baking powder

1 teaspoon finely chopped fresh chives

3 tablespoons vegetable fat or lard

1 Heat the oil in a large saucepan. When it is hot, add the onion, garlic and thyme. Sauté for 2–3 minutes, stirring occasionally. Add the chunks of pork and cook for 10 minutes until browned.
2 Add the chopped tomatoes, cooked lentils and tomato purée. Pour in the vegetable stock, bring to the boil and then simmer for 10 minutes.
3 Meanwhile, to make the dumplings, place all the dumpling ingredients in a mixing bowl and rub together until the mixture resembles fine breadcrumbs. Add 1 tablespoon cold water and mix until a stiff dough is formed, adding a little extra water if needed. Roll the dough into 24 small balls.
4 Add the cubes of sweet potato to the soup, then add the dumplings and stir. Continue cooking the soup over a low heat for a further 20 minutes. Sprinkle with chopped fresh parsley and serve immediately.

parsleyed ham and leeks with puff pastry

SERVES 4 • PREP 25 MINS, PLUS COOLING • COOK 50–55 MINS • CALS PER PORTION 820 • FAT PER PORTION 45 G

450 g (1 lb) new potatoes, scrubbed

25 g (1 oz) butter

3 leeks, sliced

125 g (4 oz) peas

175 g (6 oz) cooked ham, diced

500 g (1 lb 2 oz) packet puff pastry

1 egg, beaten

1 handful of mustard seeds

For the parsley sauce:

25 g (1 oz) butter

25 g (1 oz) flour

300 ml (½ pint) milk

2 tablespoons chopped fresh parsley

1 Cook the new potatoes in a large saucepan of boiling water for 10 minutes, drain and cool. Cut them in half and set aside.
2 Melt the butter in a saucepan and add the leeks. Sauté gently until soft but not browned. Cook the peas in a small saucepan of boiling water for 3 minutes, drain and set aside.
3 To make the parsley sauce, heat the butter until melted, then remove from the heat and stir in the flour. Add a little of the milk and stir well. Add the rest of milk and return to the heat, stirring continuously until the sauce begins to thicken. Remove from the heat, stir in the parsley and season well with salt and black pepper. Add the potatoes, leeks, peas and ham to the sauce and spoon the mixture into a 1.1 litre (2 pint) pie dish. Allow to cool.
4 Preheat the oven to gas mark 6/200°C (400°F). Roll out the pastry on a floured surface and dampen the edges of the pie dish with water. Cut narrow strips of pastry and lay them around the top edge of the dish. Dampen them with water then top with a lid of pastry. Pinch the edges of pastry together to seal, then trim.
5 Brush the pastry with beaten egg and sprinkle with mustard seeds. Bake in the oven for 30 minutes until golden.

mushroom, brie and pancetta salad

SERVES 4 • PREP 5 MINS • COOK 10 MINS • CALS PER PORTION 380 • FAT PER PORTION 35 G

4 large brown cap mushrooms, such as portobello

150 g (5 oz) Brie, cut into 4 slices

4 sprigs of fresh thyme

250 g (9 oz) packet spinach

ground black pepper

For the dressing:

125 g (4 oz) pancetta or streaky bacon, diced

4 tablespoons olive oil

2 tablespoons balsamic vinegar

50 g (2 oz) black olives, pitted and chopped

1 To make the dressing, fry the pancetta or bacon until crispy, remove from the pan and drain on kitchen paper. In a bowl, combine the olive oil, balsamic vinegar, pancetta and black olives. Set aside.

2 Cook the mushrooms under a preheated grill for 5 minutes until cooked. Top each mushroom with a slice of Brie and a sprig of thyme and season well with freshly ground black pepper. Grill for a further 2 minutes until the cheese has melted.

3 To serve, divide the spinach between 4 plates, drizzle over the dressing and place the mushrooms on top.

chicken pot pie

SERVES 4 • PREP 45 MINS • COOK 45 MINS • CALS PER PORTION 950 • FAT PER PORTION 52 G

1 Melt the butter in a large saucepan. Add the shallots and bay leaf and cook for 4–5 minutes over a low heat until soft. Add the carrots and celery, and cook for a further 5–7 minutes.

2 Remove the bay leaf, sprinkle over the flour and cook, stirring, for a further 1–2 minutes. Remove from the heat and gradually add the stock, stirring until smooth, then cook over a low heat for 3–4 minutes until thickened.

3 Add the chicken chunks and frozen peas, then season well with salt and ground black pepper. Divide the chicken mixture among four 450 ml (¾ pint) ovenproof dishes or deep soup bowls.

4 Preheat the oven to gas mark 5/190°C (375°F). Roll out the pastry on a clean, floured surface until 5 mm (¼ in) thick. Cut out four circles, one and a half times larger than the diameter of the pie dishes. Wet the underneath edge of each circle and stretch the pastry over each pie dish, sealing the edges against the dish to make a lid.

5 Make a small slit in the top of the pastry lid with a sharp knife. Brush the pastry with beaten egg and bake in the oven for 45 minutes until golden.

50 g (2 oz) butter

3 shallots, sliced

1 bay leaf

2 carrots, peeled and diced

2 celery sticks, finely sliced

25 g (1 oz) flour

450 ml (¾ pint) chicken stock

700 g (1½ lb) cooked chicken, cut into chunks

75 g (3 oz) frozen peas

500 g (1 lb 2 oz) packet shortcrust pastry

1 medium egg, beaten

chicken and tomato ragout

SERVES 4 • PREP 15 MINS • COOK 45 MINS • CALS PER PORTION 330 • FAT PER PORTION 19 G

1 Preheat the oven to gas mark 6/200°C (400°F). Place the tomatoes, sugar, shallots and oil in a roasting tin. Season with salt and ground black pepper and stir to coat well.
2 Carefully lift the skin from each chicken leg, separating it from the meat, and stuff each cavity using 2 tablespoons of the parsley. Rub the chicken legs with salt and pepper, and lay them on top of the ingredients in the roasting tin.
3 Roast in the oven for 40 minutes until the chicken is cooked. If the pan gets too dry add 150 ml (¼ pint) boiling water.
4 In a small bowl or mortar, combine the remaining parsley, lemon zest and garlic to make gremolata, an Italian seasoning which perfectly complements the ragout. Stir it into the chicken, breaking up the tomatoes and combining the juices. Return the ragout to the oven for 5 minutes, then serve.

900 g (2 lb) plum tomatoes, halved

1 teaspoon caster sugar

150 g (5 oz) shallots, peeled and trimmed

2 tablespoons olive oil

4 chicken legs

3 tablespoons roughly chopped fresh parsley

grated zest of 1 lemon

1 garlic clove, crushed

chicken curry

SERVES 4 • PREP 10 MINS • COOK 40 MINS • CALS PER PORTION 280 • FAT PER PORTION 13 G

1 Heat the oil in a large frying pan, add the onion and garlic and fry gently for 10 minutes until softened and golden. Add the turmeric, chilli powder, ground coriander and cumin and cook for 1 minute, stirring.
2 Add the tomatoes and season with salt. Bring to the boil, cover and simmer for 20 minutes.
3 Add the cooked chicken to the frying pan with the garam masala and 4 tablespoons of the yogurt. Cover and cook gently for 10 minutes, then stir in the rest of the yogurt. If desired, serve the curry with basmati rice and naan bread.

2 tablespoons oil

1 large onion, chopped

2 garlic cloves, finely chopped

1 teaspoon turmeric

½ teaspoon chilli powder

1½ teaspoons ground coriander

1½ teaspoons ground cumin

3 tomatoes, quartered

550 g (1¼ lb) cooked chicken, skinned and cut into chunks

1 teaspoon garam masala

150 ml (¼ pint) thick plain yogurt

chicken tikka salad

SERVES 4 • PREP 10 MINS • COOK NONE • CALS PER PORTION 165 • FAT PER PORTION 10 G

15 g (½ oz) packet fresh mint, roughly chopped

15 g (½ oz) packet fresh coriander, roughly chopped

1 red onion, finely sliced

100 g (3½ oz) packet rocket

300 g (11 oz) ready-cooked chicken tikka pieces

2 poppadums, broken into pieces

For the dressing:

170 g (approx 6 oz) tub tzatziki

1 teaspoon coriander seeds, crushed

1 To make the dressing, mix together the tzatziki and coriander seeds, season with salt and ground black pepper and set aside.
2 Toss together the mint and fresh coriander, the onion, rocket and chicken pieces. Top with the poppadum pieces and spoon over the dressing. Serve immediately.

Variation

You can improve the presentation of the chicken salad by using small individual mini poppadums instead of larger poppadums broken into pieces.

chicken tikka kebabs with minted yogurt

SERVES 5, MAKES 10 KEBABS • PREP 10 MINS • COOK NONE • CALS PER PORTION 260 • FAT PER PORTION 14 G

1 Cut the chicken fillets into wedges and slide onto ten wooden skewers, alternating them with lime wedges and onion slices.
2 Mix the mint jelly with the yogurt and serve with the cold kebabs as a dip.

2 x 210 g (approx 7 oz) packets cooked mini chicken tikka fillets

2 limes, cut into small wedges

1 red onion, roughly sliced

2 tablespoons mint jelly

500 g (1 lb 2 oz) tub Greek yogurt

roast chicken and vegetable kebabs

SERVES 4 • PREP 20 MINS, PLUS MARINATING • COOK 10 MINS • CALS PER PORTION 430 • FAT PER PORTION 31 G

400 g (14 oz) casserole vegetables, such as onion, carrot, swede, turnip and parsnip, peeled and cut into small chunks

6 tablespoons tapenade

4 sprigs of fresh rosemary

8 tablespoons olive oil

4 skinless, boneless chicken breasts, cut into 2.5 cm (1 in) cubes

1 Parboil all the casserole vegetables, except the onion, in a saucepan of boiling, salted water, for 5 minutes, then drain well.

2 In a large bowl, mix together the tapenade, rosemary sprigs and 6 tablespoons of the olive oil. Add the cubes of chicken, vegetable chunks and onion and stir to coat them in the mixture. Cover and chill in the fridge for at least 30 minutes, preferably overnight, to absorb the flavours.

3 Skewer the chicken and vegetables onto eight metal skewers. Place them under a preheated hot grill and cook for 10 minutes, turning halfway, until crispy.

4 Drizzle the cooked kebabs with the remaining olive oil and serve with a feta cheese salad (see page 119).

all-in-one roast

SERVES 4 • PREP 20 MINS • COOK 1 HR • CALS PER PORTION 500 • FAT PER PORTION 18 G

1 Preheat the oven to gas mark 6/200°C (400°F). Put the potatoes, parsnips, carrots, shallots, lemon juice, 1 tablespoon roughly chopped sage and the olive oil in a bowl. Season with salt and ground black pepper. Stir to coat thoroughly.

2 Using a sharp knife, score three shallow cuts in each chicken breast. Put a sage leaf into each cut and place the chicken in a large roasting tin. Leaving the shallots until later, arrange the potatoes, parsnips and carrots around the chicken and drizzle over any remaining liquid.

3 Roast for 45 minutes, stirring the vegetables halfway through. Add the shallots and roast for a final 15 minutes.

2 large potatoes, peeled and cut into small chunks

3 parsnips, peeled and cut into small chunks

225 g (8 oz) carrots, peeled and cut into small chunks

300 g (11 oz) shallots, peeled and trimmed

juice of 1 lemon

15 g (½ oz) packet fresh sage

2 tablespoons olive oil

4 large chicken breasts

Tip
For an easy way to peel shallots, place them in a bowl of hot water, leave for a few minutes then skin.

turkey and ham cakes

SERVES 4 • PREP 10 MINS, PLUS CHILLING • COOK 10 MINS • CALS PER PORTION 500 • FAT PER PORTION 24 G

500 g (1 lb 2 oz) mashed potato

125 g (4 oz) cooked ham, chopped

250 g (9 oz) turkey, cooked and chopped

15 g (½ oz) packet fresh parsley, chopped

2 tablespoons double cream

75 g (3 oz) strong cheddar, grated

2 teaspoons Dijon mustard

flour, for coating

1 egg, beaten

75 g (3 oz) fresh breadcrumbs

2 tablespoons vegetable oil

25 g (1 oz) butter

1 In a large mixing bowl combine the potato, ham, turkey, chopped parsley, cream, cheese and mustard, using enough cream to bind the mixture together. Mix thoroughly and season with salt and ground black pepper.
2 Divide the mixture into eight and shape into round cakes with floured hands. Chill in the fridge for at least 1 hour until firm.
3 When ready to cook, dip the cakes lightly in flour, then in beaten egg, then coat in breadcrumbs.
4 Heat the oil and butter in a frying pan, add the cakes and shallow fry for 4–5 minutes on each side. If desired, serve with a crisp green salad and a spoonful of cranberry relish.

turkey broth with noodles and mint

SERVES 6 • PREP 15 MINS • COOK 40 MINS • CALS PER PORTION 250 • FAT PER PORTION 4 G

1 Place the onion, carrot, leek, bay leaves, peppercorns, thyme, parsley and tomatoes into a large pan or flameproof casserole and cover with 1.7 litres (3 pints) water. Season well with salt and black pepper. Bring to the boil and simmer gently for 30 minutes.

2 Add the udon or egg noodles to a large saucepan of boiling water and cook according to packet instructions. Drain, then leave them in cold water.

3 After 30 minutes, remove the vegetables and herbs from the stock with a slotted spoon and discard.

4 Add the cooked noodles, mint, coriander, turkey, green beans and flageolet beans to the pan and simmer gently. Season well with salt and pepper and serve in soup bowls.

1 onion, halved

1 carrot, cut into chunks

1 leek, cut into chunks

4 bay leaves

1 handful of black peppercorns

1 bunch of fresh thyme

1 small bunch of fresh parsley

2 tomatoes, halved

150 g (5 oz) udon or egg noodles

1 handful of fresh mint leaves, chopped

1 handful of fresh coriander, chopped

400 g (14 oz) cooked turkey, shredded

125 g (4 oz) green beans, cooked

400 g (14 oz) can flageolet beans, drained and rinsed

turkey with baby roast potatoes
and green herb sauce

SERVES 8 • PREP 15 MINS • COOK 25 MINS • CALS PER PORTION 270 • FAT PER PORTION 15 G

1 kg (2¼ lb) baby new potatoes

2 tablespoons olive oil

70 g (approx 3 oz) packet chorizo sausage, sliced

250 g (9 oz) French beans, cut at one end only

2 large cooked turkey breasts, legs or leftover turkey, skinned and roughly sliced

pinch of sea salt

For the green herb sauce:

1 bunch of fresh parsley, roughly torn

1 bunch of fresh basil, roughly torn

2 tablespoons white wine vinegar

5 tablespoons olive oil

2 garlic cloves, finely chopped

Tip
This is a good way of using up leftover turkey. The green herb sauce will keep in the fridge for up to a week.

1 Preheat the oven to gas mark 6/200°C (400°F). Place the potatoes in a large saucepan of cold water and bring to the boil, simmer for 4 minutes, then drain and allow to cool.
2 Put the potatoes on a baking tray, drizzle with 1 tablespoon of the oil and sprinkle with salt. Bake for 15 minutes until golden. Fry the chorizo in the remaining oil until crispy. Set aside.
3 Add the French beans to a small saucepan of boiling, salted water and cook for 2 minutes. Drain and set aside.
4 Combine the sauce ingredients in a food processor or blender.
5 Arrange the turkey, chorizo and vegetables in a serving bowl and toss with the sauce, or serve in a separate bowl.

7

fish and seafood

Fish and seafood are high in omega-3, which helps prevent heart disease. As fish is so good for us and quick to cook, it makes ideal after-work suppers. Choosing quality fish and seafood is probably the most important element; look for a firm flesh, bright eyes and gills, and a fresh smell.

salmon fishcakes with garlic mayonnaise

SERVES 4 • PREP 10 MINS • COOK 30 MINS • CALS PER PORTION 750 • FAT PER PORTION 49 G

1 Put the potatoes in a saucepan of cold salted water and bring to the boil. Simmer, covered, for 20 minutes until cooked. Drain and mash roughly with a fork.

2 Meanwhile, put the salmon fillet in a saucepan and cover with the milk. Add a little salt and the whole black peppercorns. Bring the milk to the boil and simmer for 10 minutes. Remove the fish from the pan with a slotted spoon and remove the skin from the fish while still warm. Break the fish into chunks, ensuring that all the bones are removed in the process.

3 Mix together the cooked potatoes, flaked salmon, shallots, dill, lemon zest and juice in a large bowl. Season with salt and ground black pepper. Divide the mixture into eight and shape each portion into a fishcake.

4 Coat the fishcakes lightly with flour. Heat the vegetable oil in a large frying pan. Fry the fishcakes in batches for 3–4 minutes on each side until golden and cooked through.

5 Meanwhile, combine the ingredients for the garlic mayonnaise then serve it with the fishcakes.

550 g (1¼ lb) floury potatoes, peeled and halved

700 g (1½ lb) salmon fillet, with skin

600 ml (1 pint) milk

4 black peppercorns

3 shallots, finely chopped

2 tablespoons roughly chopped fresh dill

grated zest and juice of 1 lemon

25 g (1 oz) plain flour

4 tablespoons vegetable oil

For the mayonnaise:

2 garlic cloves, crushed

1 tablespoon capers, roughly chopped

1 teaspoon Dijon mustard

4 tablespoons mayonnaise

Variation
Use a combination of salmon and cod, instead of just salmon, if preferred.

salmon and cream cheese pancakes

SERVES 8–10 • PREP 10 MINS • COOK NONE • CALS PER PORTION 500–400 • FAT PER PORTION 46–36 G

3 x 200 g (7 oz) tubs cream cheese

6 tablespoons whipping cream

3 ready-made plain pancakes

2 x 200 g (7 oz) packets oak-smoked Scottish salmon

juice of 1 lemon

1 bunch of fresh chives, chopped

1 In a mixing bowl combine all of the cream cheese with the whipping cream.

2 To assemble the pancakes, lay one pancake flat and spread it with one-third of the cream cheese mixture. Place half of the smoked salmon evenly over the cream cheese and season with ground black pepper and half of the lemon juice.

3 Top with a second pancake and repeat, then top with the final pancake. Using a palette knife, carefully spread the remaining cream cheese mixture over the top and around the sides of the stack of pancakes then cover with the chopped chives. Chill for 1 hour then serve.

Variation

For a meaty alternative to fish, replace the salmon with slices of salami and use roughly chopped flat leaf parsley instead of chives.

salmon en croûte
with mushrooms, leeks and tarragon

SERVES 8 • PREP 35 MINS, PLUS CHILLING • COOK 45–50 MINS, PLUS RESTING • CALS PER PORTION 660 • FAT PER PORTION 42 G

1 To make the filling, heat the oil in a large pan, add the leeks and mushrooms and cook for 5–10 minutes, until liquid has been absorbed. Add the crème fraîche and tarragon. Season and add lime zest. Cook for 1 minute, then remove and leave to cool.
2 Take one packet of pastry and roll it out on a lightly floured surface into a rectangle about 4 cm (1½ in) larger all round than the salmon fillets. Roll out the pastry in the second packet into a rectangle larger than the first one by 5 cm (2 in) all round.
3 Lay the smaller rectangle of pastry on a well-floured baking tray. Place one salmon fillet in the centre. Spoon the mushroom and leek filling over the fillet then place the second fillet on top.
4 Brush the pastry around the salmon with beaten egg and lay the second pastry piece on top, without stretching. Press lightly around the outside of the salmon, taking care not to trap too much air inside, then press the pastry edges together well.
5 Trim the edges of the pastry to leave a 2.5 cm (1 in) band. Mark the edges with a fork and decorate the top by gently pressing an upturned teaspoon into the pastry, working in rows. Brush once more with egg. Chill for 1 hour. Preheat the oven to gas mark 6/200°C (400°F) and pop a baking tray in the oven to heat.
6 Remove the salmon en croûte from the fridge. Brush again with beaten egg then carefully slide it onto the hot baking tray. Bake for 35–40 minutes until golden. Leave to rest for 5 minutes. Serve in slices, with new potatoes and a green salad if desired.

2 x 350 g (12 oz) packets shortcrust pastry, chilled

2 x 550 g (1¼ lb) pieces of fresh, skinned salmon fillet

1 egg, beaten, to glaze

For the filling:

2 tablespoons olive oil

200 g (7 oz) leeks, washed and sliced into rings

225 g (8 oz) mushrooms, sliced

200 ml (7 fl oz) tub low-fat crème fraîche

4 tablespoons roughly chopped fresh tarragon

grated zest of 1 lime

haddock, salmon and pepper kebabs

MAKES 6 SKEWERS • PREP 20 MINS, PLUS SOAKING SKEWERS AND MARINATING • COOK 8–10 MINS •
CALS PER SKEWER 315 • FAT PER SKEWER 24 G

150 ml (¼ pint) olive oil

1–2 garlic cloves, roughly chopped

2 tablespoons lemon juice

1 teaspoon fennel seeds, crushed

450 g (1 lb) haddock fillets, skinned and cut into 12 chunks

250 g (9 oz) salmon fillets, cut into 6 chunks

1 onion

1 large green pepper, cored, deseeded and roughly chopped into 12 pieces

½ large red pepper, cored, deseeded and roughly cut into 6 pieces

1 lemon, cut into 6 wedges

1 Soak six bamboo skewers in cold water for 30 minutes. In a food processor, whizz together the oil, garlic, lemon juice and fennel seeds to make a marinade. Place the fish in a shallow dish, coat in the marinade, then cover and chill for at least 30 minutes, or overnight.

2 Cut the onion into six wedges, cutting through the root so that the layers remain intact. Bring a saucepan of water to the boil, add the onion, bring back to the boil and simmer for 1 minute. Then add the pieces of green and red pepper and simmer for 1 further minute until just tender. Drain the vegetables, plunge into cold water, allow to cool and then drain again.

3 Thread the onions, peppers, haddock, salmon and lemon onto the six soaked skewers. Season with salt and black pepper and brush with the leftover marinade. Cook the kebabs on a barbecue or under a preheated oven grill for 8–10 minutes or until the fish is cooked, turning once and brushing again with the marinade.

lemon cod stew

SERVES 4 • PREP 15 MINS • COOK 25 MINS • CALS PER PORTION 270 • FAT PER PORTION 2 G

1 Pour the fish stock into a large saucepan and bring to the boil. Add the cubed potatoes and grated lemon zest, and simmer for 10 minutes. Add the quartered tomatoes and sliced leeks and continue to simmer for 5 minutes.

2 Cut the cod into thick slices and add to the saucepan. Cook for a further 10 minutes until the fish is cooked, the potatoes are soft and the liquid has reduced and thickened slightly.

3 Season generously with salt and ground black pepper and then serve in bowls, sprinkled with the basil.

450 ml (¾ pint) fish stock

2 large baking potatoes, peeled and cut into small cubes

grated zest of 2 lemons

450 g (1 lb) plum tomatoes, roughly quartered

225 g (8 oz) baby leeks, sliced

500 g (1 lb 2 oz) skinless, boneless chunky cod

1 tablespoon roughly chopped fresh basil

Variation
For a cheaper alternative to cod, use huss or whiting.

cod with crumble topping

SERVES 1 • PREP 10 MINS • COOK 8 MINS • CALS PER PORTION 150 • FAT PER PORTION 5 G

100 g (3½ oz) piece of cod fillet, skinned

1 teaspoon groundnut oil

1 tablespoon oatmeal or dried breadcrumbs

1 tablespoon chopped fresh parsley

grated zest and juice of 1 lemon

1 Brush the cod fillet on both sides with oil.

2 In a bowl, mix together the oatmeal or breadcrumbs, parsley, lemon zest and season with salt and ground black pepper. Press the crumble mixture onto both sides of the cod to coat.

3 Heat a non-stick frying pan and cook the cod for 4 minutes on each side, or place under a preheated grill if preferred.

4 Sprinkle the cod with lemon juice just before serving.

chilli-glazed cod

SERVES 2 • PREP 5 MINS • COOK 5 MINS • CALS PER PORTION 240 • FAT PER PORTION 2 G

1 red chilli, deseeded and
finely chopped

2 teaspoons soy sauce

grated zest and juice of 1 lime

pinch of ground allspice

50 g (2 oz) soft brown sugar

2 x 175 g (6 oz) thick cod fillets

1 In a small mixing bowl mix together the red chilli, soy sauce, lime zest and juice, allspice and soft brown sugar.

2 Cook the cod fillets under a preheated grill for 1 minute on each side. Remove from the grill, coat with the chilli glaze and grill for 2–3 minutes more.

3 Serve, with mashed potatoes and steamed greens if desired.

spiced sweet potato and fish pie

SERVES 4 • PREP 25 MINS • COOK 30 MINS • CALS PER PORTION 340 • FAT PER PORTION 8 G

4 haddock fillets, each about 150 g (5 oz)

125 g (4 oz) thick Greek yogurt

225 g (8 oz) sweet potatoes, peeled and roughly diced

450 g (1 lb) potatoes

150 ml (¼ pint) semi-skimmed milk

2 teaspoons coriander seeds, crushed

150 g (5 oz) cooked peeled prawns

2 large spring onions, sliced

1 teaspoon yellow mustard seeds

Tip
It's important to use a rich yogurt in this dish – a low-fat version will make it watery. You could also use crème fraîche.

1 Preheat the oven to gas mark 6/200°C (400°F). Place the haddock in a bowl and mix with 4 tablespoons of the Greek yogurt. Tip into a roasting tin, cover with foil and bake in the oven for 10–15 minutes, or until just cooked through.

2 Meanwhile, fill a large saucepan with water and add the sweet potatoes, potatoes and 1 teaspoon salt. Cover and bring to the boil. Simmer gently for about 15 minutes until cooked through, then drain and mash with the milk and coriander seeds. Add plenty of salt and pepper.

3 Flake the cooked fish into a 1.1 litre (2 pint) oval ovenproof dish, removing any skin or bones. Add the prawns and scatter over the spring onions and yellow mustard seeds. Spoon over the remaining yogurt and season well with salt and black pepper.

4 Top the fish mixture with the mash, spreading it evenly to the edges of the dish. Bake for 20–30 minutes, until the top of the pie begins to colour. Serve, with a crisp watercress salad if desired.

plaice with feta and lemon

SERVES 4 • PREP 10 MINS • COOK 5 MINS • CALS PER PORTION 270 • FAT PER PORTION 20 G

1 Tuck under both ends of each half of plaice fillet and put onto a lightly oiled baking tray. Cook under a preheated grill for 5 minutes until cooked.

2 Meanwhile, heat the olive oil in a heavy-based frying pan or griddle pan. Fry the courgette slices for 3 minutes until they start to brown slightly. Remove from the pan and lay on absorbent kitchen paper to drain.

3 In a bowl, mix together the feta cheese, olives, thyme and courgette strips. In another bowl, mix the dressing ingredients and season well with salt and ground black pepper. Drizzle the dressing over the feta cheese salad. Divide the salad among four plates and place the cooked fish on top. Serve immediately.

4 x 75 g (3 oz) plaice fillets, skinned, rinsed and halved lengthways

1 tablespoon olive oil

3 courgettes, sliced lengthways into ribbons using a vegetable peeler

125 g (4 oz) feta cheese, cubed

125 g (4 oz) black olives, pitted

3 sprigs of fresh thyme, stripped

For the dressing:

1 teaspoon lemon juice

2 tablespoons olive oil

skate with caper berries
and mustard green lentils

SERVES 4 • PREP 5 MINS • COOK 10 MINS • CALS PER PORTION 375 • FAT PER PORTION 16 G

4 x 200 g (7 oz) pieces of skate, rinsed

75 g (3 oz) butter, plus extra for greasing

1 bay leaf

12 caper berries, or capers

juice of ½ lemon

410 g (approx 14 oz) can green lentils

1 teaspoon wholegrain mustard

1 Place the pieces of skate on a lightly buttered baking tray and cook under a preheated grill for 5 minutes each side.

2 Meanwhile, add the butter and bay leaf to a small frying pan. Heat until bubbling and turning slightly brown, then season with salt and ground black pepper. Stir in the caper berries and lemon juice and simmer for 1 minute.

3 Heat the lentils in a saucepan, season well and then stir in the wholegrain mustard. Divide the lentils among four plates, top each with a piece of skate and pour over the hot caper berry sauce. Serve immediately.

Tip
Skate has a wonderful meaty taste and needs very little cooking. It's also great value for money. Don't be put off by its strange appearance – skate really is worth trying.

pan-fried oat-crusted mackerel
with apple and red onion relish

SERVES 4 • PREP 10 MINS • COOK 20 MINS • CALS PER PORTION 590 • FAT PER PORTION 41 G

1 To make the relish, heat 1 tablespoon of the oil in a large heavy-based frying pan. Gently fry the onion and apple wedges for 5–6 minutes until soft and starting to caramelize.

2 Meanwhile, using a sharp pair of scissors, snip the tail and fins off the mackerel. Brush the fish with a little of the oil and then coat the fish in the oats.

3 Heat the remaining oil in another large frying pan and fry the fish for 10–15 minutes, turning halfway, until crisp and cooked. Serve with the warm apple and onion relish.

4 tablespoons olive oil

1 red onion, cut into wedges

2 large red apples, cored and cut into wedges

4 large mackerel, topped and tailed

75 g (3 oz) oats

smoked mackerel and potato salad

SERVES 4 • PREP 10 MINS • COOK 20–25 MINS • CALS PER PORTION 540 • FAT PER PORTION 43 G

500 g (1 lb 2 oz) new potatoes

200 ml (7 fl oz) tub crème fraîche

2 teaspoons creamed horseradish sauce

15 g (½ oz) packet fresh dill, finely chopped

2 sweet cucumber spears, roughly chopped

4 spring onions, finely sliced

4 smoked mackerel fillets, flaked

1 Cook the potatoes in a large saucepan of boiling water for 20–25 minutes until cooked. Drain and cool.
2 In a small bowl, combine the crème fraîche, horseradish, dill, cucumber spears and spring onions. Add the potatoes, coat them in the dressing then gently fold in the flaked mackerel. Season well with salt and ground black pepper, and serve.

Variations

If you cannot find smoked mackerel, replace it with smoked trout or, for a more delicate flavour, try grilled salmon pieces, flaked.

tuna niçoise

SERVES 4 • PREP 5 MINS • COOK 10 MINS • CALS PER PORTION 380 • FAT PER PORTION 20 G

1 Add the green and broad beans to a large saucepan of boiling, salted water and cook for 2 minutes. Drain and plunge in cold water so that they retain their colour. Drain and set aside.

2 In a bowl, mix together the chopped anchovies, if using, the spring onions, cherry tomatoes, boiled new potatoes and cooked beans, then gently fold in the quartered hard-boiled eggs. In a separate bowl, mix together the dressing ingredients and season with salt and ground black pepper.

3 Cook the tuna steaks under a preheated hot grill for about 5 minutes each side.

4 Divide the salad among four plates and drizzle with a little dressing. Lay a tuna steak on top of each salad and pour over the remaining dressing. Garnish with basil leaves.

150 g (5 oz) packet extra fine green beans, trimmed

125 g (4 oz) fresh or frozen broad beans

6 anchovy fillets, roughly chopped (optional)

3 spring onions, thickly sliced

200 g (7 oz) cherry tomatoes, halved

225 g (8 oz) new potatoes, boiled

2 hard-boiled eggs, quartered

4 x 150 g (5 oz) tuna steaks

fresh basil leaves, to garnish

For the dressing:

3 tablespoons olive oil

1 tablespoon lemon juice

1 tablespoon chopped fresh basil

Variation

For a cheaper alternative to fresh tuna steaks, use a 400 g (14 oz) can tuna. Drain, flake and mix with the salad.

tagliatelle marinara

SERVES 4 • PREP 10 MINS • COOK 20 MINS • CALS PER PORTION 430 • FAT PER PORTION 3 G

400 g (14 oz) dried tagliatelle

1 onion, finely chopped

1 garlic clove, crushed

400 g (14 oz) can chopped tomatoes with herbs

1 handful of freshly chopped parsley

225 g (8 oz) packet frozen mixed seafood, defrosted

1 Cook the pasta in a large saucepan of boiling, salted water according to packet instructions.

2 Meanwhile, in a non-stick pan, dry-fry the onion and garlic until soft. Add the chopped tomatoes, parsley and defrosted mixed seafood. Heat through and season with salt and ground black pepper, before serving with the cooked drained tagliatelle.

kedgeree

SERVES 8 • PREP 30 MINS • COOK 20 MINS • CALS PER PORTION 420 • FAT PER PORTION 13 G

1 Place the haddock in a large saucepan with the milk and simmer gently for about 5 minutes until the fish is cooked. Drain, reserving the poaching liquid. Roughly flake the fish, discarding any bones that you find.

2 Add the rice, flaked haddock, coriander seeds, hard-boiled eggs, double cream, chives and reserved poaching liquid to a large frying pan. Season with salt and ground black pepper. Stir and simmer gently for 5 minutes then add the parsley.

3 To make the lime butter, melt the butter in a small pan and stir in the lime juice and a little seasoning. Pour over the kedgeree, garnish with lime zest and serve.

900 g (2 lb) smoked undyed haddock, skinned

300 ml (½ pint) milk

450 g (1 lb) basmati rice, cooked

1 teaspoon coriander seeds, crushed

3 hard-boiled eggs, quartered

4 tablespoons double cream

3–4 tablespoons chopped fresh chives

½ bunch of fresh parsley, chopped

For the lime butter:

50 g (2 oz) butter

2 tablespoons lime juice

grated zest of lime, to garnish

dijon mussels

SERVES 4 • PREP 15 MINS • COOK 10 MINS • CALS PER PORTION 200 • FAT PER PORTION 12 G

25 g (1 oz) unsalted butter

2 shallots, finely chopped

2 garlic cloves, crushed

150 ml (¼ pint) dry white wine

1 kg (2¼ lb) mussels in shells, cleaned

50 ml (2 fl oz) double cream

3 tablespoons Dijon mustard

1 handful of fresh chives, chopped

1 Melt the butter in a saucepan large enough to hold the mussels, and gently fry the shallots and garlic until soft. Add the white wine and bring to the boil.

2 Add the mussels, discarding any open ones, cover the pan with a tight-fitting lid and cook over a moderate heat for 4–5 minutes until the mussel shells have opened. Discard any unopened ones.

3 Strain the cooking liquid through a sieve into a small pan. Add the cream and mustard and bring to the boil.

4 Transfer the mussels to four serving bowls and pour over the sauce. Serve immediately, sprinkled with fresh chives.

squid in cornmeal
and cumin

SERVES 4 • PREP 5 MINS • COOK 10 MINS •
CALS PER PORTION 280 • FAT PER PORTION 14 G

1 In a deep fat fryer or large saucepan, heat the vegetable oil to 200°C (400°F). Rinse the squid. Mix the cornmeal, cumin and salt and ground black pepper together in a shallow dish, then toss the squid rings in the mixture to coat.
2 Fry the squid, a few pieces at a time, for about 3 minutes. When golden and crisp, remove the squid from the oil with a slotted spoon and place on kitchen paper to drain.
3 Sprinkle the fried squid lightly with salt and serve immediately with lime wedges and tartare sauce.

Tip
To save time, get your fishmonger to prepare the squid into rings. And try to find baby squid – it's not as tough as the bigger squid.

700 g (1½ lb) fresh baby squid, ready-prepared and sliced into 5 mm (¼ in) thick rings

50 g (2 oz) cornmeal

1 teaspoon ground cumin

vegetable oil, for deep frying

lime wedges and tartare sauce, to serve

sesame prawns

SERVES 4 • PREP 10 MINS • COOK NONE • CALS PER PORTION 300 • FAT PER PORTION 10 G

4 tablespoons sesame seeds

2 tablespoons chilli flakes

250 g (9 oz) cooked tiger prawns

320 g (approx 11½ oz) jar plum sauce, to serve

1 In a bowl, mix together the sesame seeds and chilli flakes.
2 Dip the shelled prawns in the mixture until well coated, and serve with the plum sauce.

mediterranean grilled sardines

SERVES 4 • PREP 10 MINS • COOK 6–8 MINS • CALS PER PORTION 380 • FAT PER PORTION 24 G

16 sardines, cleaned

olive oil, for drizzling

1 Place the sardines under a preheated grill and cook for 3–4 minutes each side.

2 Drizzle over a little olive oil and serve, with lemon wedges, fresh bread and a basil and tomato salad if desired.

vegetarian

Eating veggie food is great for your health, whether you have converted to vegetarianism totally or you just want to create a meat-free meal or two in the week. It is also an economical way to eat and there's a vast array of fruit, vegetables, nuts and pulses to try. Just make sure you get the right balance so you get all the nutrients you need.

quick minestrone

SERVES 4 • PREP 15 MINS • COOK 20 MINS • CALS PER PORTION 200 • FAT PER PORTION 70 G

2 tablespoons olive oil

1 celery stick, chopped

1 small onion, chopped

1 red pepper, cored, deseeded and cut into 5 mm (¼ in) pieces

2 garlic cloves, crushed

6 tomatoes, seeded and cut into 5 mm (¼ in) pieces

1 tablespoon chopped thyme

425 ml (14½ fl oz) hot vegetable stock

110 g (3¾ oz) small pasta shapes

½ Savoy cabbage, shredded

freshly grated Parmesan

1 Heat the olive oil in a large saucepan. Add the celery and onion and cook for 5 minutes. Add the red pepper, garlic, tomatoes and thyme. Season with salt and ground black pepper, then stir well and cook, covered, for a further 5 minutes until soft.
2 Pour in the hot stock, increase the heat and bring to the boil. Add the pasta and cabbage and cook for 5–6 minutes until cooked. Serve immediately with the grated Parmesan on top.

Tip
Use a 400 g (14 oz) can chopped tomatoes instead of the fresh tomatoes, if preferred. Simply drain and add as above, increasing the cooking time at the end of Step 1 to 10 minutes.

root vegetable crisps

SERVES 6–8 • PREP 15 MINS • COOK 15 MINS • CALS PER PORTION 300–222 • FAT PER PORTION 19–14 G

1 Finely slice each vegetable lengthways.
2 Heat the sunflower oil in a deep fat fryer to 180°C (350°F).
3 Carefully fry the vegetable strips in manageable batches for 2–3 minutes until crisp. Remove with a slotted spoon, drain on kitchen paper and sprinkle with sea salt.

2 potatoes

2 sweet potatoes

2 small parsnips

3 carrots

1 aubergine, trimmed

sunflower oil, for frying

stuffed artichokes

SERVES 4 • PREP 25 MINS, PLUS COOLING • COOK 40–45 MINS • CALS PER PORTION 220 • FAT PER PORTION 13 G

1 Hold each artichoke firmly and snap the stalk, pulling out the tough, stringy strands. Using a sharp knife, cut off the top third of each artichoke and snip off the point of any outer leaves with kitchen scissors. Rub lemon halves over the artichokes to stop them discolouring, and squeeze the remaining juice into a large saucepan of boiling, salted water.

2 Add the artichokes to the pan and boil for 30 minutes. They are cooked when an outer leaf can easily be pulled off. Plunge the artichokes into cold water to cool. Drain upside down.

3 Remove the central cone of leaves and the hairy central choke from each artichoke with a teaspoon. Preheat the oven to gas mark 5/190°C (375°F).

4 Meanwhile make the filling. In a large, heavy-based saucepan, heat 1 tablespoon of the oil and gently fry the onion and garlic for 5 minutes until soft. Add the tomatoes and olive paste and continue to heat for 10 minutes until reduced to a thick purée.

5 Remove from the heat, stir in the breadcrumbs and capers and season with salt and ground black pepper. Use the mixture to fill the centre of the artichokes and then sprinkle with Parmesan.

6 Place the stuffed artichokes in a roasting tin, drizzle with the remaining oil and bake in the oven for 10 minutes to reheat. Serve the artichokes garnished with a sprinkling of parsley.

4 x 300 g (11 oz) artichokes

1 lemon, halved

2 tablespoons chopped fresh flat leaf parsley, to garnish

For the filling:

3 tablespoons olive oil

1 onion, finely chopped

1 garlic clove, crushed

400 g (14 oz) can chopped tomatoes

1 tablespoon olive paste

2 tablespoons white breadcrumbs

1 tablespoon capers

50 g (2 oz) Parmesan, grated

tabbouleh

SERVES 8 • PREP 15 MINS • COOK NONE • CALS PER PORTION 240 • FAT PER PORTION 12 G

1 Put the bulgar wheat and a pinch of salt in a mixing bowl and cover with boiling water. Stir and leave for 15 minutes. When the bulgar wheat is plump, drain and squeeze out as much water as you can, then put to one side.
2 Mix the olive oil and lemon juice, and season with salt and pepper. Add to the bulgar wheat and stir, then mix in the fresh herbs.
3 Add the garlic, cucumber, tomatoes and spring onions, and toss.

Vegetarian tips
• Don't just swap meat for cheese to get your daily intake of proteins - eggs, beans, nuts, peas and pulses all contain protein
• Eat hard cheeses rather than soft if you're counting the calories
• Calcium-rich soya milk can be substituted for cow's milk
• Try eating seasonal fruit and vegetables - it will save you money and you will notice a real difference in the flavour
• As meat is the main source of iron in most people's diets you must eat more beans, lentils, green, leafy vegetables and dried fruits to make sure that you don't become anaemic
• Small quantities of fat will not only provide vitamins A, D and E, but will also add flavour to your cooking. Use unsaturated types, such as olive oil, for healthier meals
• Make your own muesli using nuts and dried fruits for a healthy, nutrition-packed start to the day.

275 g (10 oz) bulgar wheat

125 ml (4 fl oz) olive oil

125 ml (4 fl oz) lemon juice

2 bunches of mint, finely chopped

1 large bunch of fresh flat leaf parsley, finely chopped

3 garlic cloves, crushed

1 cucumber, diced

6 tomatoes, diced

1 bunch of spring onions, chopped

chickpea and pitta salad

SERVES 8 • PREP 10 MINS • COOK 5 MINS • CALS PER PORTION 390 • FAT PER PORTION 9 G

2 x 425 g (15 oz) cans chickpeas, drained and rinsed

1 cucumber, diced

2 chillies, deseeded and sliced

1 bunch of fresh parsley, finely chopped

For the croûtons:

1 packet 10 small round pitta breads

2 tablespoons olive oil

For the dressing:

2 tablespoons olive oil

juice of 1 lemon

2 teaspoons wholegrain mustard

2 garlic cloves, crushed

1 Preheat the oven to gas mark 4/180°C (350°F).

2 To make the croûtons, split the pitta breads in half then cut them into small triangles. Place on a baking tray and drizzle with the olive oil. Bake in the oven for 5 minutes until toasted.

3 Mix together all the dressing ingredients and set aside.

4 Put the chickpeas, cucumber, chillies and parsley in a bowl and toss with the dressing. Sprinkle with the pitta croûtons.

panzanella salad

SERVES 4 • PREP 10 MINS • COOK 5 MINS, PLUS RESTING • CALS PER PORTION 411 • FAT PER PORTION 20 G

1 Preheat the oven to gas mark 6/200°C (400°F). Place the ciabatta cubes on a baking tray. Place in the oven and bake for 5 minutes until dry and crispy.
2 In a large bowl, toss the tomatoes, ciabatta cubes, artichokes, cucumber and capers together, then season with salt and ground black pepper. Drizzle over the olive oil and lemon juice. Set aside for 10 minutes to allow the flavours to combine.
3 Scatter over the chopped basil and serve this light summer salad, a speciality from Italy.

1 ciabatta loaf, cut into 2.5 cm (1 in) cubes

5 small tomatoes, quartered

285 g (approx 10½ oz) jar artichoke antipasto, drained

½ cucumber, peeled and cut into small chunks

1 tablespoon capers

4 tablespoons olive oil

juice of 1 lemon

2 tablespoons chopped fresh basil

thai vegetable salad

SERVES 4 • PREP 5 MINS • COOK 4 MINS • CALS PER PORTION 444 • FAT PER PORTION 35 G

300 g (11 oz) packet stir-fry vegetables

2 hard-boiled eggs, quartered

50 g (2 oz) peanuts, chopped

juice of 1 lime

For the peanut sauce:

400 ml (14 fl oz) can coconut milk

2 tablespoons madras curry paste

2 tablespoons crunchy peanut butter

2 tablespoons brown sugar

1 To make the peanut sauce, heat the coconut milk, curry paste, peanut butter and brown sugar in a large frying pan. Bring to the boil and then simmer for 2 minutes.

2 Meanwhile, divide the stir-fry vegetable mix among four serving bowls, add the eggs and peanuts, and drizzle over the lime juice. Season well with salt and ground black pepper. Pour over the hot peanut sauce and serve immediately.

Variations

Buying a ready-prepared stir-fry vegetable mix greatly reduces preparation time, however you can always select and prepare your own selection of vegetables if preferred. If you don't want a spicy sauce, use a milder curry paste.

winter wensleydale cheese salad

SERVES 4 • PREP 15 MINS • COOK 20 MINS • CALS PER PORTION 350 • FAT PER PORTION 24 G

1 Heat the oil in a large saucepan. Fry the parsnips for 5 minutes over a medium heat, stirring occasionally to get an even colour.
2 Add the onion and peppers and fry for a further 10 minutes.
3 In a salad bowl, toss the fried vegetables with the salad leaves and crumble the cheese over the top. Season generously with salt and lots of ground black pepper. Serve immediately, drizzled with balsamic vinegar.

Variation

If you fancy a change, replace the Wensleydale with feta cheese and serve the salad with focaccia bread for a Mediterranean feel.

2 tablespoons olive oil

300 g (11 oz) small parsnips, peeled and cut into quarters

1 red onion, cut into 8 wedges

2 red peppers, cored, deseeded and cut into 6

150 g (5 oz) packet Italian-style salad leaves

200 g (7 oz) Wensleydale cheese, crumbled

1–2 tablespoons balsamic vinegar

roasted vegetables

SERVES 6 • PREP 15 MINS • COOK 35–40 MINS • CALS PER PORTION 160 • FAT PER PORTION 6 G

700 g (1½ lb) salad potatoes, unpeeled and halved

1 head of garlic, divided into cloves, with skins left on

4 sprigs of fresh rosemary

3 tablespoons olive oil

2 green peppers, cored, deseeded and roughly chopped

2 large courgettes, cut into chunks

300 g (11 oz) packet baby vine tomatoes

sea salt

1 Preheat the oven to gas mark 7/220°C (425°F). Put the potatoes, whole garlic cloves and rosemary in a large roasting tin. Drizzle with 2 tablespoons of the olive oil and roast for 10 minutes.

2 Add the peppers and courgettes, sprinkle with ½ teaspoon salt and the remaining olive oil, and cook for another 15–20 minutes until the vegetables are beginning to char at the edges.

3 Lay the baby vine tomatoes on top of the vegetables and cook for a final 10 minutes until their skins start to split, the vegetables are charred and the potatoes are cooked.

baked goats' cheese parcels

SERVES 6 • PREP 5 MINS • COOK 15–20 MINS • CALS PER PORTION 200 • FAT PER PORTION 19 G

1 Preheat the oven to gas mark 4/180°C (350°F) or prepare an outdoor barbecue.
2 Place each goats' cheese on a 10 x 10 cm (4 x 4 in) square of foil and pull up the sides. Drizzle 1 tablespoon oil over each cheese and top with a sprig of thyme. Fold the edges of the foil together to seal the parcels and cook for 15–20 minutes in the oven or on the barbecue, until the cheese begins to melt.
3 Drizzle the cheeses with extra oil and serve with toasted bread.

6 hard goats' cheeses, at room temperature

6 tablespoons olive oil, plus a little extra for drizzling

6 sprigs of fresh thyme

baked garlic

SERVES 6 • PREP 5 MINS • COOK 25–30 MINS • CALS PER PORTION 45 • FAT PER PORTION 4 G

2 whole heads of garlic

olive oil, for drizzling

ground black pepper

1 Preheat the oven to gas mark 4/180°C (350°F) or prepare an outdoor barbecue. Put the garlic in a pan of boiling water. Bring to the boil, simmer gently for 5 minutes then drain. When cooled slightly, cut the tops off the heads of garlic to reveal the cloves.
2 Place each head of garlic on a 10 x 10 cm (4 x 4 in) square of foil. Drizzle 1 tablespoon oil over each and season with black pepper.
3 Wrap in foil and cook in the oven for 15–20 minutes or on a barbecue for 25–30 minutes, until tender. Remove the flesh from the cloves, spread on toast and serve with goats' cheese parcels (see above).

daal

SERVES 4 • PREP 5 MINS • COOK 20 MINS • CALS PER PORTION 230 • FAT PER PORTION 4 G

250 g (9 oz) red split lentils

200 g (7 oz) can chopped tomatoes

2 fresh green chillies, deseeded and chopped

¼ teaspoon ground turmeric

1 teaspoon grated fresh root ginger

1 tablespoon vegetable oil

2 teaspoons black mustard seeds

2 garlic cloves, sliced

1 tablespoon chopped fresh coriander

1 Bring the lentils to the boil in a saucepan of water, spooning off any scum on the surface, and then simmer for 30 minutes. Add the tomatoes, chillies, turmeric and ginger and simmer gently for a further 5 minutes. Season with salt and pepper.
2 In a small frying pan heat the oil and fry the mustard seeds and garlic for 1–2 minutes until the mustard seeds pop. Remove from the heat and pour onto the daal. Stir and serve hot, garnished with chopped coriander.

Tip
For convenience, replace the red split lentils with a 400 g (14 oz) can of cooked red lentils.

cheddar and spinach soufflé

SERVES 2 • PREP 15 MINS • COOK 25 MINS • CALS PER PORTION 640 • FAT PER PORTION 50 G

1 Preheat the oven to gas mark 7/220°C (425°F). Use a little of the butter to grease two 600 ml (1 pint) ramekin or soufflé dishes. Divide the Parmesan between the dishes, coating the insides thoroughly. Tap out the excess cheese and discard.

2 Heat the remaining butter in a heavy-based pan, add the nutmeg and spinach, and lightly cook for 2 minutes to wilt the spinach. Remove the spinach from the pan, press it against a sieve to remove any liquid and chop it roughly.

3 Whisk the egg yolks and wine in an ovenproof bowl set over a saucepan of simmering water for 5–10 minutes until pale and thick. Add the cheddar and spinach, and season generously with salt and ground black pepper.

4 In a separate bowl, whisk the egg whites until stiff. Fold a small amount into the spinach, then carefully fold in the rest.

5 Spoon the mixture into the prepared dishes and run a blunt knife around the inside of the rims to remove excess mixture from the sides and allow the soufflés to rise smoothly. Place in the oven and bake for 25 minutes until golden and puffy. Serve immediately, with fresh bread and a crisp green salad if desired.

25 g (1 oz) butter

2 tablespoons finely grated Parmesan

½ teaspoon nutmeg

225 g (8 oz) young spinach leaves, trimmed and stalks removed

4 eggs, separated

50 ml (2 fl oz) dry white wine

125 g (4 oz) apple wood-smoked cheddar, grated

courgette and stilton cannelloni

SERVES 4 • PREP 20 MINS • COOK 5 MINS • CALS PER PORTION 800 • FAT PER PORTION 66 G

50 g (2 oz) butter

1 onion, finely chopped

1 large courgette, grated

350 ml (12 fl oz) double cream

8 sheets of fresh lasagne

125 g (4 oz) blue Stilton

1 tablespoon chopped fresh thyme

1 In a heavy-based pan, melt the butter and gently fry the onion. Add the courgette and fry for 5 minutes. Pour in the cream, reserving 2 tablespoons, and boil rapidly until it has reduced by half. Season with salt and ground black pepper.

2 Meanwhile, cook the lasagne sheets in a large saucepan of boiling, salted water, according to packet instructions. Drain well and set aside.

3 Spoon a generous tablespoon of the courgette mixture onto a lasagne sheet. Lift and roll into a tube. Repeat with the rest of the pasta and the filling.

4 Place the prepared cannelloni in a buttered shallow dish. Pour over the reserved cream, crumble the Stilton on top, sprinkle over the thyme and place under a preheated hot grill for a few minutes until the cheese has melted.

red pepper tortilla

SERVES 6 • PREP 10 MINS • COOK 25 MINS • CALS PER PORTION 300 • FAT PER PORTION 19 G

1 In a 23 cm (9 in) cast-iron deep frying pan with vertical sides, heat the oil until very hot. Add the potatoes and onion. Stir and soften but don't allow to brown. Add the pepper and tomatoes and spread evenly.
2 Add the vegetable stock to the eggs, season with salt and black pepper and pour over the potato mixture, coating it well.
3 Cook over a high heat, shaking the pan occasionally. When the top is solid and cooked, place under a preheated grill until golden. Cut into slices and serve the tortilla hot or cold.

Variation

This delicious tortilla of fried potatoes, red pepper and tomato can also include leftovers, such as mushrooms or sausages.

100 ml (3½ fl oz) olive oil

3 potatoes, sliced

1 onion, sliced

1 red pepper, cored, deseeded and thinly sliced

4 tomatoes, cut into wedges

3 tablespoons vegetable stock

6 eggs, beaten

carrot and parsnip tart tatin

SERVES 4 • PREP 25 MINS • COOK 30 MINS • CALS PER PORTION 750 • FAT PER PORTION 44 G

1 Preheat the oven to gas mark 5/190°C (375°F).

2 Melt the butter in a cast-iron frying pan. Sauté the carrots and parsnips until they begin to colour slightly. Sprinkle with the sugar and cook until golden. Add 1 tablespoon water and stir to produce a syrup; add the honey and stir gently. Remove from the heat and leave to cool.

3 Roll out the pastry on a lightly floured surface and sprinkle with the mustard powder. Place the pastry on top of the vegetables and tuck it in to cover.

4 Place the pan in the oven and bake for 20 minutes until the pastry is golden. Allow to cool for 5 minutes, then turn out onto a plate, so that the tart is now upside down.

50 g (2 oz) butter

3 large carrots, peeled and cut lengthways

3 parsnips, peeled and cut lengthways

1 tablespoon demerara sugar

1 tablespoon honey

500 g (1 lb 2 oz) packet shortcrust pastry

2 teaspoons mustard powder

red onion, thyme and olive pizza

SERVES 4 • PREP 25 MINS, PLUS RISING • COOK 10–15 MINS • CALS PER PORTION 290 • FAT PER PORTION 8 G

1 Sift the flour, salt and yeast onto a flat work surface. Make a well in the middle and pour in 150 ml (¼ pint) warm water and 1 tablespoon of the oil. Using your hands, gradually mix to form a soft dough, then knead until smooth. Place the ball of dough in an oiled bowl, cover with a tea towel and leave in a warm place for 1 hour until doubled in size.

2 Heat 1 tablespoon of the oil in a pan and gently cook the red onions until softened. Preheat a baking tray in the oven set to gas mark 8/230°C (450°F).

3 Roll out the dough thinly on a lightly floured surface to a rectangle about 35.5 x 23 cm (14 x 9 in). Top with the onions, olives and thyme. Drizzle with the remaining olive oil and slide onto the preheated baking tray. Bake for 10–15 minutes until cooked and golden. Serve immediately with a drizzle of olive oil.

225 g (8 oz) strong plain white flour

½ teaspoon salt

7 g (¼ oz) sachet fast-action dried yeast

3 tablespoons olive oil

4 red onions, cut into wedges

75 g (3 oz) pitted black olives

½ tablespoon chopped fresh thyme or sprigs of fresh thyme

easy puff pastry mushroom pie

SERVES 6 • PREP 30 MINS • COOK 30 MINS • CALS PER PORTION 470 • FAT PER PORTION 36 G

2 onions, roughly chopped

2 tablespoons olive oil

350 g (12 oz) brown cap
mushrooms, quartered

200 g (7 oz) tub crème fraîche

2 tablespoons finely chopped
fresh thyme

100 g (3½ oz) green olives,
roughly chopped (optional)

500 g (1 lb 2 oz) packet puff
pastry or 2 x 375 g (13 oz)
packets ready-rolled puff pastry

1 egg, beaten

1 tablespoon wholegrain
mustard

1 Preheat the oven to gas mark 6/200°C (400°F).
2 In a large frying pan, cook the onions in the oil for 5 minutes
until golden. Add the mushrooms and cook for 10 minutes more,
stirring from time to time. Season with salt and black pepper.
Add the crème fraîche, thyme and olives, if using, and cook over
a high heat for a further 2 minutes until the cream is reduced.
3 Roll out the pastry on a lightly floured work surface into two
35.5 x 20 cm (14 x 8 in) rectangles, or use ready-rolled pastry
rolled to the same measurement. Lay one piece on a lightly
floured baking tray and spread with the mushroom mixture,
leaving a 2.5 cm (1 in) rim around the edges.
4 Brush the rim with the beaten egg and lay the second rectangle
of pastry on top. Squeeze the pastry edges together to seal.
Brush the top with the remaining beaten egg and the mustard.
Bake for 30 minutes until cooked and golden.

vegetable curry

SERVES 2 • PREP 20 MINS • COOK 20 MINS • CALS PER PORTION 715 • FAT PER PORTION 31 G

1 Heat the vegetable oil in a frying pan. Add the French beans and mushrooms and stir-fry for 2 minutes.
2 Add the curry sauce, cover the pan and cook for 10 minutes, then stir in the spinach until it wilts.
3 Meanwhile, cook the rice according to packet instructions. Drain and rinse well.
4 Divide the cooked rice between two plates. Top with the curry and serve accompanied by half a naan bread each.

2 tablespoons vegetable oil

100 g (3½ oz) French beans, trimmed

100 g (3½ oz) mushrooms

350 g (12 oz) jar vegetarian curry sauce

100 g (3½ oz) baby spinach, trimmed and stalks removed

100 g (3½ oz) basmati rice

1 large naan bread

vegetarian toad-in-the-hole
with horseradish and sage

SERVES 4 • PREP 15 MINS, PLUS RESTING • COOK 40–45 MINS • CALS PER PORTION 370 • FAT PER PORTION 14 G

125 g (4 oz) plain flour

1 egg

300 ml (½ pint) milk

1 tablespoon horseradish sauce

1 tablespoon roughly chopped
fresh sage

1 tablespoon olive oil

8 vegetarian sausages

1 red onion, roughly sliced

250 g (9 oz) brussels sprouts

Variations

Use up any leftover cooked
vegetables and vary the herbs
for a different flavour. Mustard
seasoning, instead of the
horseradish, will work just
as well. You can use pork
sausages for meat eaters.

1 Put the flour and a pinch of salt into a bowl, add the egg and a
little milk and stir. Add the remaining milk and continue stirring
until all the flour is combined. Add the horseradish sauce and
the sage and season with ground black pepper. Whisk well with
a fork, beating out any lumps. Leave the batter to rest in the
fridge for 30 minutes.

2 Preheat the oven to gas mark 7/220°C (425°F). Heat the olive
oil in a large frying pan. Lightly fry the sausages and red onion
for 5 minutes.

3 Meanwhile, cook the brussels sprouts in a saucepan of boiling
water for 5 minutes. Drain, add to the frying pan and cook for
2 minutes until lightly browned.

4 Layer the sausages, onion and sprouts in an ovenproof dish
and pour over the chilled batter. Place in the oven and bake for
20–25 minutes until golden.

sweet tooth

Go on, indulge yourself. Whether you love gooey cakes,
ice cream or fruity desserts, here is something for you.
When making desserts, and especially cakes, stick strictly
to the recipe – this is one area of cookery that needs to be
followed to the letter – and have all your equipment ready.
Weighing up all ingredients beforehand is also a good idea.

strawberry semi-freddo

SERVES 6 • PREP 20 MINS, PLUS FREEZING • COOK 10 MINS • CALS PER PORTION 533 • FAT PER PORTION 38 G

1 Line a 23 x 12.5 cm (9 x 5 in) loaf tin with clear film.

2 In a heavy-based saucepan, gently heat 300 ml (½ pint) water with 175 g (6 oz) of the caster sugar until dissolved. Bring to the boil and continue to heat for 5 minutes until reduced by half and the mixture is a light syrup.

3 Add the strawberries to the syrup, remove from the heat and allow to cool. Crush the strawberries slightly with a fork; strain and reserve the juice. Put the strawberries to one side.

4 In a heatproof bowl set over a saucepan of boiling water, whisk together the egg yolks and remaining sugar until pale in colour and doubled in volume.

5 In another bowl, whisk the cream until stiff. Fold in the egg mixture then the reserved juice until combined. Pour the mixture into the prepared loaf tin, level out and freeze for 1 hour.

6 Remove from the freezer, gently push the strawberries evenly into the mixture. Freeze for 4 hours. Remove from the freezer 20 minutes before serving.

250 g (9 oz) caster sugar

225 g (8 oz) strawberries, hulled

4 egg yolks

450 ml (¾ pint) double cream

hazelnut and strawberry pavlova

SERVES 8 • PREP 20 MINS • COOK 2 HRS, PLUS DRYING • CALS PER PORTION 420 • FAT PER PORTION 24 G

6 egg whites

350 g (12 oz) caster sugar

2 teaspoons cornflour

1 teaspoon balsamic vinegar

1 tablespoon ground hazelnuts

For the topping:

284 ml (approx ½ pint) carton double cream, lightly whipped

225 g (8 oz) strawberries, hulled and halved

50 g (2 oz) roasted hazelnuts, chopped

1 Preheat the oven to gas mark ½/120°C (250°F). Cut out a 20.5 cm (8 in) circle of non-stick greaseproof paper and place it on a baking tray.

2 To make the meringue, whisk the egg whites in a grease-free bowl until very stiff, then gradually whisk in the caster sugar, adding it a tablespoon at a time. You should be able to turn the bowl upside down and the meringue will not drop out!

3 Beat the cornflour and balsamic vinegar into the meringue. Using a metal spoon, gently fold in the ground hazelnuts.

4 Spoon the meringue mixture onto the greaseproof paper, around the edge of the circle, shaping each spoonful into an oval. Place a spoonful in the centre and flatten slightly. Add a second layer of meringue, putting smaller spoonfuls around the edge.

5 Place the meringue in the oven and bake for 2 hours until firm, then leave to cool in the oven for 4 hours without opening the door. Remove the paper from the base of the meringue and put the meringue on a plate. Pile with whipped double cream and strawberries and sprinkle with chopped hazelnuts.

lemon sorbet

200 g (7 oz) caster sugar

grated zest and juice of
3 lemons

1 sprig of fresh rosemary

SERVES 8 • PREP 5 MINS • COOK 5 MINS, PLUS COOLING AND FREEZING •
CALS PER PORTION 100 • FAT PER PORTION 0 G

1 In a large heavy-based saucepan, gently heat 1 litre (1¾ pints) water with the sugar until dissolved. Add the lemon zest and juice and the rosemary and bring to the boil. Remove from the heat and plunge the base of the pan into cold water for 15 minutes.
2 Pass the liquid through a sieve, pour into a 1.3 litre (2¼ pint) plastic tub and freeze for 4 hours, or until the mixture is almost frozen solid at the sides and bottom, but still liquid in the middle.
3 Empty the contents of the tub into a large chilled bowl and whisk vigorously or whizz in a food processor for 5 minutes.
4 Return the sorbet mixture to the plastic tub and freeze it for 4 hours or overnight, until solid. Remove from the freezer about 30 minutes before serving.

summer fruits granita

500 g (1 lb 2 oz) packet frozen mixed summer fruits, defrosted

125 g (4 oz) caster sugar

4 blackcurrant, vanilla and ginseng tea bags

150 ml (¼ pint) vodka

SERVES 8 • PREP 10 MINS, PLUS COOLING AND FREEZING • COOK 15 MINS •
CALS PER PORTION 110 • FAT PER PORTION 0 G

1 In a heavy-based saucepan, gently heat the summer fruits, sugar and 1 litre (1¾ pints) water until the sugar has dissolved. Add the tea bags, increase the heat and simmer for 10 minutes until the fruit is soft.
2 Remove from the heat and plunge the base of the pan into cold water for 15 minutes. Remove the tea bags.
3 Put the mixture into a blender and whizz until smooth. Pass through a sieve to make a purée.
4 Pour the purée into a 1.1 litre (2 pint) plastic tub, stir in the vodka and freeze for 6 hours, or until the granita mixture is almost frozen solid at the sides and bottom, but still liquid in the middle. Empty the contents of the plastic tub into a large chilled bowl and stir thoroughly.
5 Return the mixture to the plastic tub and freeze for 4 hours, or overnight, until solid. Serve straight from the freezer and use a fork to break up the ice crystals.

coconut and lime ice cream

SERVES 8 • PREP 10 MINS, PLUS FREEZING • COOK NONE • CALS PER PORTION 175 • FAT PER PORTION 4 G

400 ml (14 fl oz) can low-fat coconut milk, chilled

500 g (1 lb 2 oz) tub low-fat fromage frais

juice of 1 lime

200 g (7 oz) icing sugar

1 In a large chilled bowl, mix together the coconut milk, fromage frais, lime juice and icing sugar until smooth.

2 Pour the mixture into a 1.1 litre (2 pint) plastic tub. Freeze for about 4 hours, or until the mixture is almost frozen at the sides and bottom, but still liquid in the middle.

3 Empty the contents of the tub into a large chilled bowl and whisk vigorously or whizz in a food processor for 5 minutes.

4 Return the mixture to the tub and freeze for 4 hours or overnight, until solid. Remove 30 minutes before serving.

easy summer pudding

SERVES 4 • PREP 15 MINS, PLUS DEFROSTING • COOK NONE • CALS PER PORTION 420 • FAT PER PORTION 32 G

450 g (1 lb) packet frozen mixed summer fruits, such as blackberries or blueberries

3 teaspoons sugar

4 croissants, sliced in half lengthways

200 g (7 oz) tub crème fraîche

1 Allow the frozen fruit to defrost in a sieve set over a bowl. When defrosted, reserve the juice collected in the bowl and stir half of the sugar into the fruit.

2 Place the croissants in four dessert bowls. Spoon the reserved fruit juice over the croissants and leave for about 10 minutes until the bread has absorbed all the juice.

3 Pile the fruit on top of each slice, sprinkle with the remaining sugar, then spoon over the crème fraîche and serve.

Tip
If you prefer to use mixed fresh berries rather than frozen, you will need 200 ml (7 fl oz) cranberry and blackcurrant juice.

white chocolate brioche pudding

SERVES 6 • PREP 15 MINS, PLUS RESTING AND DRYING OUT • COOK 30–40 MINS • CALS PER PORTION 960 • FAT PER PORTION 63 G

1 Put the chocolate, milk, cream and caster sugar in a heatproof bowl set over a saucepan of simmering water. Cook over a low heat, stirring, until the chocolate has melted. Cool and set aside.
2 Mix the egg and yolks together and gradually whisk in the white chocolate mixture until combined.
3 Put the blueberries in the bottom of a 1.7 litre (3 pint) ovenproof dish, then add the brioche. Pour over half of the chocolate custard mixture, leave for 30 minutes, then pour over the remaining custard mixture.
4 Preheat the oven to gas mark 4/180°C (350°F). Stand the filled dish in a roasting tin and add enough hot water to the tin so that it comes at least halfway up the sides of the dish. Place in the oven and bake the pudding for 30–40 minutes until the custard is set in the centre. Carefully place under a preheated grill to brown. Serve warm or at room temperature.

Tips
Use good-quality white chocolate for this recipe. If you can't find brioche, you can replace it with a 125 g (4 oz) sliced baguette.

200 g (7 oz) white chocolate, broken into small pieces

200 ml (7 fl oz) semi-skimmed milk

568 ml (approx 1 pint) carton double cream

50 g (2 oz) caster sugar

1 egg, plus 5 egg yolks

75 g (3 oz) blueberries

400 g (14 oz) brioche loaf, cut into 5 mm (¼ in) slices and dried out for 2–3 hours

christmas pudding

SERVES 8 • PREP 40 MINS • COOK 2 HRS, PLUS A FURTHER 1½ HRS OR 10 MINS IN MICROWAVE •
CALS PER PORTION 700 • FAT PER PORTION 26 G

125 g (4 oz) white breadcrumbs

175 g (6 oz) plain flour with pinch of salt added

½ teaspoon each ground ginger, cinnamon and nutmeg

1 teaspoon mixed spice

75 g (3 oz) shredded vegetable suet

225 g (8 oz) dark muscovado sugar

125 g (4 oz) mixed citrus peel, finely chopped

175 g (6 oz) currants

125 g (4 oz) sultanas

225 g (8 oz) raisins

75 g (3 oz) prunes, chopped

125 g (4 oz) semi-dried cranberries

50 g (2 oz) almonds, blanched and halved

125 g (4 oz) pecans, chopped

125 g (4 oz) peeled, diced apples

grated zest and juice of 1 lemon and 1 orange

4 tablespoons each French brandy and cider

3 eggs, beaten

1 tablespoon black treacle

2 tablespoons milk (optional)

1 Lightly grease a 1.1 litre (2 pint) pudding bowl and line the base with a circle of greaseproof paper. Place all the dry ingredients in a large mixing bowl and stir well until combined.

2 In a separate bowl, mix together the lemon and orange juice, the brandy and cider, and beat in the eggs. Pour the liquid mixture into the dry ingredients and mix thoroughly. Stir in the treacle. Add the milk if the mixture isn't wet enough – it should drop off a spoon easily.

3 Tightly pack the mixture into the pudding basin and cover with a double sheet of greaseproof paper, pleated in the middle. Wrap a double length of string around the bowl and secure with a knot, leaving a long length of string for a handle. Overwrap with foil, tucking the ends under the pleated greaseproof paper. Pull the remaining string over the basin and loop under the string to form a handle, tie a knot and trim excess string and paper.

4 Pour boiling water into a large lidded saucepan and lower the pudding into it. Cover and simmer for 2 hours, topping up with boiling water as necessary. Allow to cool for 30 minutes, then discard the foil and paper. Cover with clean greaseproof paper and foil, and store in a cool, dry place for up to 3 months.

5 On the day of serving, steam for 1½ hours or reheat in the microwave for 10 minutes, then leave to rest before turning out.

easy foolproof custard

SERVES 2 • PREP 5 MINS • COOK 10 MINS • CALS PER PORTION 270 • FAT PER PORTION 11 G

300 ml (½ pint) milk

1 bay leaf and a pinch of ground nutmeg

2 egg yolks

50 g (2 oz) caster sugar

2 teaspoons cornflour

1 Heat the milk in a saucepan with the bay leaf and nutmeg until almost boiling.
2 In a mixing bowl, whisk together the egg yolks, caster sugar and cornflour until smooth. Gradually stir the hot milk into the egg mixture until smooth.
3 Sieve the warm liquid into a clean saucepan. Heat gently until the custard thickens – it is ready when it coats the back of a wooden spoon.

lemon and lime soufflé

SERVES 6 • PREP 1 HR, PLUS CHILLING • COOK NONE • CALS PER PORTION 380 • FAT PER PORTION 30 G

2 teaspoons powdered gelatine

4 eggs, separated

125 g (4 oz) caster sugar

grated zest and juice of
2 lemons to make up 100 ml
(3½ fl oz) juice (top up with
lime juice if needed)

300 ml (½ pint) double cream

grated zest of 1 lime

25 g (1 oz) pistachio nuts,
chopped

1 Cut a double strip of greaseproof paper, long enough to go around a 1.1 litre (2 pint) soufflé dish and wide enough to stand about 5 cm (2 in) above the rim. Lightly oil the greaseproof paper above the rim to make it easier to peel off. Wrap it around the outside of the soufflé dish, slightly overlapping the ends, and secure with string.

2 Pour 3 tablespoons water into a large bowl and sprinkle over the gelatine, set aside and leave to soften for 10 minutes.

3 In a separate bowl, whisk the egg yolks and sugar together for about 2 minutes until they begin to thicken. Add the 100 ml (3½ fl oz) lemon juice and whisk for 2–3 minutes. In another mixing bowl, whisk the cream until it just holds its shape, then cover and refrigerate.

4 Place the bowl of gelatine over a saucepan of simmering water until it dissolves. Pour the hot gelatine from a height into the creamy egg mixture, stirring continuously.

5 Stand the bowl containing the lemony egg mixture in a large bowl of ice-cold water. Using a spatula, stir constantly for about 5–10 minutes until it begins to thicken. Remove the bowl from the water and fold in the cream and lemon and lime zest.

6 In a large grease-free bowl, whisk the egg whites until they are firm and standing up in peaks. Add a spoonful to the lemon and lime mixture and stir, then gently fold in the remainder using a large metal spoon. Pour the mixture into the soufflé dish, shake to level the top and place it in the fridge to set for 2–3 hours.

7 Remove the greaseproof paper and decorate with the pistachio nuts, pressing them gently around the edge of the soufflé.

sweet almond risotto

SERVES 4 • PREP 10 MINS • COOK 2 HRS • CALS PER PORTION 540 • FAT PER PORTION 21 G

1.1 litres (2 pints) milk

2 tablespoons double cream

200 g (7 oz) pudding rice

2 tablespoons caster sugar

½ vanilla pod, slit open with seeds scraped out

grated zest of ½ orange, plus extra for decorating

25 g (1 oz) ground almonds

1 handful of toasted flaked almonds, to decorate

1 Preheat the oven to gas mark 3/160°C (325°F).

2 In an ovenproof dish, mix together the milk, double cream, pudding rice, caster sugar, vanilla pod, grated orange zest and the ground almonds.

3 Place the dish in the oven and bake for 2 hours, until the rice is tender, stirring the rice after 30 minutes.

4 Remove the rice pudding from the oven. Allow to cool for a few minutes then top with grated orange zest and the toasted flaked almonds. Serve warm.

foolproof pancakes

MAKES 10–12 PANCAKES • PREP 5 MINS • COOK 20 MINS • CALS PER PANCAKE 80–70 • FAT PER PANCAKE 3–2 G

125 g (4 oz) plain flour, sifted

1 egg, beaten

300 ml (½ pint) milk

1 tablespoon sunflower oil

1 Put the flour in a bowl and make a well in the centre. Add the egg. Gradually beat in half of the milk, stirring in the flour. As the mixture starts to thicken, add in the remaining milk. Beat until the batter is smooth and creamy.

2 In a small, heavy-based frying pan, heat a little of the oil. When the oil is really hot, add a ladleful of batter – enough to cover the base of the pan thinly. Tilt the pan to form an even layer of batter and cook for 1 minute. Turn the pancake over with a palette knife and cook for 1 minute more. Tip the pancake onto a plate and keep warm while you use the remaining batter to make more pancakes in the same way.

3 Serve the pancakes hot with your favourite topping.

Tip

The secret of a deliciously light pancake is how you cook it. Don't put too much batter in the pan and don't use a lot of fat or oil.

baklava

SERVES 12 • PREP 30 MINS • COOK 40 MINS • CALS PER PORTION 390 • FAT PER PORTION 22 G

12 sheets of filo pastry

75 g (3 oz) butter, melted

75 g (3 oz) pistachio nuts, shelled and chopped

411 g (approx 14½ oz) jar mincemeat

grated zest of 1 orange

1 tablespoon honey (optional)

For the almond paste:

75 g (3 oz) butter

125 g (4 oz) golden caster sugar

50 g (2 oz) plain flour

150 g (5 oz) ground almonds

1 Preheat the oven to gas mark 3/160°C (325°F).
2 To make the almond paste, whizz the butter, caster sugar, flour, ground almonds and 1 tablespoon water in a food processor for 1–2 minutes, or beat in a bowl with a wooden spoon. The mixture will be quite crumbly. Set aside.
3 To assemble the baklava, lay two sheets of filo pastry in the bottom of a 20.5 cm (8 in) square tin. Trickle melted butter over the pastry, then sprinkle over one-sixth of the pistachio nuts and layer with one-fifth of the mincemeat, almond paste and orange zest. Repeat the layering of pastry, melted butter, pistachio nuts, mincemeat, almond paste and orange zest until you have six layers of pastry, ending with a pastry layer.
4 Brush the top pastry layer with melted butter and top with the remaining pistachio nuts. Slice the baklava into triangles and bake in the oven for 30 minutes until golden. Serve drizzled with honey if desired.

raisin scones

MAKES 8 • PREP 25 MINS • COOK 40–45 MINS • CALS PER SCONE 420 • FAT PER SCONE 18 G

375 g (13 oz) plain flour

2 teaspoons cream of tartar

1 teaspoon bicarbonate of soda

½ teaspoon ground nutmeg

125 g (4 oz) butter

1 medium egg

150 ml (¼ pint) half-fat cream

125 g (4 oz) caster sugar

100 g (3½ oz) raisins

milk, for brushing

1 Preheat the oven to gas mark 6/200°C (400°F).

2 In a food processor, whizz the flour, cream of tartar, bicarbonate of soda, nutmeg and butter. Add the egg, cream and sugar. Pulse briefly until the dough comes together. Don't overprocess and allow it to toughen.

3 Turn out the scone mixture onto a clean, floured work surface and gently fold in the raisins, being careful not too handle the dough too much.

4 Using a floured rolling pin, roll the dough into a 20.5 cm (8 in) round, 2.5 cm (1 in) thick. Using a knife, score the dough into eight wedges. Place the scored round on a baking tray and brush with milk. Place in the oven and bake for 40–45 minutes until slightly risen and golden brown.

drop scones

MAKES 24 • PREP 5 MINS • COOK 10 MINS • CALS PER SCONE 40 • FAT PER SCONE 1 G

1 Mix together the flour, salt and sugar in a bowl. Add the egg and gradually beat in the milk to make a thick batter.
2 Heat a little oil in a frying pan and drop spoonfuls of the mixture into the pan. Cook for 2–3 minutes until the undersides are golden and the tops have bubbled. Flip the scones over to the other side and allow to brown. Repeat until the batter mixture has been used up.
3 Serve warm. If desired, drizzle the drop scones with honey and pistachio nuts, and serve with a dollop of Greek yogurt.

Tip
The batter can be prepared the night before, covered and left to chill in the fridge.

125 g (4 oz) self-raising flour

pinch of salt

50 g (2 oz) caster sugar

1 egg

75 ml (3 fl oz) milk

oil, for frying

toffee apples

MAKES 8 • PREP 2 MINS • COOK 15 MINS • CALS PER APPLE 275 • FAT PER APPLE 0 G

1 Push a wooden lollipop stick into the core of each apple.
2 Put the granulated sugar in a small saucepan, together with
150 ml (¼ pint) water, and heat gently until dissolved. Bring to
the boil and cook for about 5 minutes until the syrup turns a
golden caramel colour, watching it carefully all the time.
3 Remove from the heat, dip the apples into the syrup mixture,
turning them to coat them evenly and then place on an oiled
baking tray until cool.

8 Cox apples, washed

450 g (1 lb) granulated sugar

chocolate truffles

MAKES 16 • PREP 20 MINS, PLUS CHILLING • COOK 5 MINS • CALS PER TRUFFLE 154 • FAT PER TRUFFLE 10 G

1 Melt the chocolate pieces in a heatproof bowl set over a saucepan of simmering water.

2 Turn off the heat. Keeping the bowl over the water, beat in the egg yolk using an electric hand whisk or a fork.

3 Heat the cream and Baileys very gently until warm, then beat into the chocolate mixture until smooth. Chill for 1–2 hours or until hard enough to roll the mixture into balls.

4 Place a generous teaspoon of the mixture into the palm of your hands and roll it gently until it forms a small ball. Next, roll it in the grated chocolate and sifted cocoa powder.

5 Arrange the truffles in a gift box, or serve on a plate.

225 g (8 oz) plain chocolate, broken into small pieces, plus another 125 g (4 oz) plain chocolate, grated

1 egg yolk, beaten

3 tablespoons double cream

2 tablespoons Baileys

75 g (3 oz) cocoa powder, sifted

hot cross buns

MAKES 12 BUNS • PREP 25 MINS, PLUS RISING • COOK 15–20 MINS • CALS PER BUN 240 • FAT PER BUN 7 G

400 g (14 oz) strong white bread flour, sifted

1 teaspoon salt

2 teaspoons mixed spice

1 teaspoon ground nutmeg

2 teaspoons ground cinnamon

50 g (2 oz) butter

150 g (5 oz) mixed dried fruit

50 g (2 oz) caster sugar

7 g (¼ oz) sachet fast-action dried yeast

2 eggs, beaten

150 ml (¼ pint) milk, slightly warmed

50 g (2 oz) shortcrust pastry

For the egg glaze:

1 egg, beaten with
1 tablespoon milk and
2 tablespoons caster sugar

1 Preheat the oven to gas mark 5/ 190°C (375°F). Sift the flour, salt and spices into a bowl, then rub in the butter. Stir in the dried fruit, sugar and fast-action dried yeast. In a separate bowl, whisk the eggs into the slightly warmed milk.

2 Make a well in the centre of the flour mixture and pour in the milk and egg mixture. Beat the ingredients together to form a soft dough, adding a little more milk if the mixture is too dry.

3 Place the dough on a lightly floured surface and knead for about 10 minutes until smooth and elastic. Put the dough in an oiled bowl, turn it over and cover with a tea towel. Leave in a warm place for ¾–1 hour until the dough has almost doubled in size.

4 Turn out the dough and knead lightly for 2 minutes. Divide it into 12 and shape into balls. Place the balls of dough on a baking tray. Using a sharp knife, make a slash in the shape of a cross on the top of each bun. Cover with a damp tea towel and leave for 35 minutes until the buns have almost doubled in size.

5 Roll out the pastry on a lightly floured surface and cut it into 9 cm (3½ in) strips. Dampen the strips with water and lay one strip across another on the top of each bun in the indentation. Brush the buns with the prepared egg glaze. Place in the oven and bake for 15–20 minutes until the buns are golden and sound hollow when tapped underneath.

cranberry muffins with orange

MAKES 12 • PREP 20 MINS • COOK 35–40 MINS • CALS PER MUFFIN 283 • FAT PER MUFFIN 12 G

150 g (5 oz) dried cranberries

grated zest and juice of 1 orange

150 g (5 oz) butter

125 g (4 oz) caster sugar

3 medium eggs, beaten

300 g (11 oz) self-raising flour, sifted

150 ml (¼ pint) full-fat milk

1 Preheat the oven to gas mark 4/180°C (350°F).
2 Place the cranberries and orange zest and juice in a small bowl and allow to soak. Meanwhile, line a muffin tin with 12 large paper cases.
3 In a large bowl, cream the butter and caster sugar together until pale and fluffy. Gradually beat in the eggs, ensuring that the mixture stays smooth. Using a large metal spoon, fold in the sifted flour. Add the milk and the soaked cranberries, and mix together until combined.
4 Carefully spoon the mixture into the muffin cases, ensuring that they are not overfull. Place the muffins in the oven and bake for 35–40 minutes until risen – the muffins are ready when they spring back when pressed lightly with the fingertips.
5 Remove the muffins from the oven and allow to cool slightly on a wire rack before serving.

shortbread

SERVES 8 • PREP 15 MINS • COOK 1 HR 10 MINS–1 HR 20 MINS • CALS PER SLICE 40 • FAT PER SLICE 1 G

1 Preheat the oven to gas 2/150°C (300°F). In a bowl beat the butter with a wooden spoon to soften it then beat in the sugar; add the flour and the semolina. Continue mixing the ingredients by hand until you have a smooth mixture that comes away from the side of the bowl and forms a ball.

2 Put the ball of dough on a floured surface, flatten it slightly with the palm of your hand then roll it out to a round to fit a shallow 20.5 cm (8 in) round cake tin, 3 cm (3¼ in) deep. Lightly press the shortbread mixture into the tin until flat, then prick with a fork all over.

3 Bake for 1 hr 10 minutes–1 hr 20 minutes until firm in the centre and golden. Remove from the oven and mark into eight slices with the back of a knife. Leave to cool for 5 minutes in the tin and then remove to a wire rack to cool completely. When cold, dredge with sugar and cut into wedges. Store in an airtight tin.

175 g (6 oz) butter, softened

75 g (3 oz) golden caster sugar

175 g (6 oz) plain flour, sifted

75 g (3 oz) semolina

golden caster sugar, for dredging

Tips
To make successful shortbread, ensure that the butter is soft. Pricking the shortbread all over will prevent it from rising in the middle.

gingerbread biscuits

MAKES 16 • PREP 25 MINS, PLUS CHILLING • COOK 15 MINS • CALS PER BISCUIT 150 • FAT PER BISCUIT 4 G

75 g (3 oz) unsalted butter

75 g (3 oz) dark brown sugar

1 egg yolk

175 g (6 oz) plain flour, sifted

2 teaspoons ground ginger

grated zest of 1 orange and
1 tablespoon orange juice

225 g (8 oz) icing sugar

1 Preheat the oven to gas mark 5/190°C (375°F).

2 In a bowl, mix together the butter and sugar until light and fluffy. Beat in the egg yolk, add the sifted flour and ginger, orange zest and juice and stir till a soft dough is formed. Wrap in clear film and chill for 1 hour.

3 Roll out the gingerbread dough on a lightly floured work surface until 5 mm (¼ in) thick. Cut out biscuits using various shaped cutters and place on a greased baking tray. Place in the oven and bake for 15 minutes until golden. Cool on a wire rack.

4 Sift the icing sugar into a bowl and gradually add 3 tablespoons boiling water. Stir until smooth. Spread the icing over the biscuits and leave to set for 1 hour.

Tips

If you are making these biscuits at Christmas and want to use them to decorate the tree, make a hole in the top with a skewer when they are still hot from oven. Allow them to cool, then tie lengths of ribbon through the holes. Alternatively, wrap the biscuits in a cellophane bag and present them as a gift.

cherry and coconut slices

SERVES 16 • PREP 15 MINS • COOK 40 MINS • CALS PER PORTION 222 • FAT PER PORTION 14 G

1 Preheat the oven to gas mark 4/180°C (350°F). Grease and line a shallow 29 x 18 x 2.5 cm (11 x 7 x 1 in) rectangular tin with greaseproof paper.
2 Cream the butter and sugar together until light and fluffy, add the eggs a little at a time, then add half of the flour.
3 Stir in the coconut and cherries and fold in the remaining flour. Spoon the mixture into the prepared tin and bake in the oven for 40 minutes until golden and a skewer inserted into the centre comes out clean. Leave in the tin for 5 minutes and then remove to a wire rack to cool completely. When cool, cut into slices.

150 g (5 oz) butter

150 g (5 oz) caster sugar

3 eggs, lightly beaten

225 g (8 oz) self-raising flour, sifted

125 g (4 oz) desiccated coconut

125 g (4 oz) naturally coloured glacé cherries, halved

Variation
Use 125 g (4 oz) chopped dried apricots instead of glacé cherries.

orange and poppy seed loaf

SERVES 8 • PREP 20 MINS • COOK 1 HR 5 MINS • CALS PER SLICE 325 • FAT PER SLICE 19 G

150 g (5 oz) self-raising flour, sifted

150 g (5 oz) caster sugar

pinch of salt

1 tablespoon grated orange zest

2 teaspoons poppy seeds

150 g (5 oz) butter, softened

3 eggs, beaten with
3 tablespoons milk

For the topping:

1 orange

2 tablespoons sugar

1 tablespoon freshly squeezed orange juice

1 Preheat the oven to gas mark 4/180°C (350°F). Line a 900 g (2 lb) loaf tin with a non-stick loaf liner, or grease the tin and line it with greaseproof paper. In a large bowl, mix together the flour, sugar, salt, orange zest and poppy seeds.

2 Add the butter and half of the egg and milk mixture and stir until well combined. Beat for 1 minute, add the rest of the egg and milk mixture and beat again for 1 minute.

3 Spoon the cake mixture into the prepared loaf tin and bake for 1 hour until a skewer inserted into the middle comes out clean. Leave to cool in the tin for 10 minutes, then remove.

4 To make the topping, pare the orange zest into fine strips and put the strips in a little hot water. Add the sugar, bring to the boil and simmer for 10 minutes until reduced. Stir in the orange juice. Allow to cool, then drizzle the topping over the cake. Serve the cake in slices as they are or spread with butter.

caramel nut tarts

SERVES 4 • PREP 10 MINS • COOK 15–20 MINS • CALS PER PORTION 400 • FAT PER PORTION 30 G

1 Preheat the oven to gas mark 6/200°C (400°F). Lay the puff pastry on a lightly floured work surface and cut out four circles measuring 11.5 cm (4½ in) in diameter.

2 Place the rounds of pastry on a lightly greased baking tray. Press one-quarter of the nuts gently into each round, leaving about 1 cm (½ in) border of pastry all round. Turn up the edges of each tart.

3 Combine the banoffee sauce and brandy, then place a spoonful of the mixture in the middle of each tart. Place the tarts in the oven and bake for 15–20 minutes or until the pastry is puffed up and cooked through. Allow to stand for 5 minutes before serving, with a scoop of best-quality vanilla ice-cream if desired.

200 g (7 oz) ready-rolled puff pastry (1 sheet)

100 g (3½ oz) hazelnuts, pecans or walnuts (or a mixture), half of them roughly chopped

4 tablespoons shop-bought banoffee sauce

2 tablespoons brandy

apple strudel

SERVES 8 • PREP 40 MINS • COOK 35–40 MINS • CALS PER PORTION 206 • FAT PER PORTION 9 G

2 large cooking apples, peeled, cored and chopped

juice of ½ lemon

grated zest of 1 lemon

50 g (2 oz) ground almonds

100 g (3½ oz) soft light brown sugar

50 g (2 oz) sultanas

½ teaspoon ground allspice

3 slices of white bread, crusts removed

4 sheets of filo pastry, cut to 40 x 29 cm (16 x 11 in) rectangles

50 g (2 oz) butter, melted

caster sugar, for sprinkling

1 Preheat the oven to gas mark 5/190°C (375°F).

2 Put the apples in a large bowl with the lemon juice and toss to coat. Add the lemon zest, ground almonds, light brown sugar, sultanas and allspice, and mix well.

3 In a food processor, whizz the bread to make fine crumbs. Lay one sheet of filo pastry on a clean tea towel. Brush with melted butter, sprinkle over one-quarter of the breadcrumbs and lay another sheet of filo on top. Repeat this layering using melted butter, breadcrumbs and pastry, finishing with the fourth sheet of filo on top.

4 Spread the apple mixture over the pastry, leaving a 5 cm (2 in) border all round. Fold the border over the apple mixture and sprinkle over the remaining breadcrumbs. With a long side of the rectangle nearest you, lift the tea towel at the corners and roll up the strudel. Stop after each roll and pat the strudel into shape.

5 Brush the top of the pastry with the remaining butter, sprinkle with caster sugar and place on a lightly greased baking tray, with the seam underneath. Place the strudel in the oven and bake for 35–40 minutes until the pastry is crispy and the apples soft. Serve in slices, with cream if desired.

chocolate and chestnut torte
with a ganache topping

SERVES 8 • PREP 25 MINS • COOK 45–50 MINS • CALS PER SLICE 770 • FAT PER SLICE 52 G

1 Preheat the oven to gas mark 4/180°C (350°F). Grease and line the base of a 20.5 cm (8 in) round, loose-bottomed deep cake tin.
2 To make the torte, put the chocolate and butter in a heatproof bowl and place it over a saucepan of gently simmering water. Stir until melted and smooth, remove from the heat and set aside.
3 Whisk the egg yolks and brown sugar in a mixing bowl until creamy. Add the Amaretto and the melted chocolate and butter mixture and stir well.
4 Add the flour to the chocolate mixture and fold in with a metal spoon until there are no traces of flour. Stir in the chestnut purée.
5 Whisk the egg whites in another bowl until stiff, then fold into the chocolate mixture using a metal spoon. Pour into the cake tin and spread evenly. Bake for 40–45 minutes, until a skewer inserted into the centre comes out clean. Leave the torte to cool in the tin for 10 minutes, then turn out onto a wire rack, remove the greaseproof paper and allow to cool completely.
6 For the ganache, pour the cream into a small saucepan and bring to the boil, then stir in the chocolate pieces until melted, stirring all the time. Leave to cool slightly then spoon over the torte and smooth with a palette knife. Decorate with the chocolate-covered almonds.

225 g (8 oz) plain chocolate, broken into small pieces

125 g (4 oz) butter, diced

3 eggs, separated

125 g (4 oz) soft brown sugar

50 ml (2 fl oz) Amaretto

75 g (3 oz) self-raising flour, sifted

250 g (9 oz) can sweetened chestnut purée

For the ganache:

284 ml (approx ½ pint) carton double cream

150 g (5 oz) plain chocolate, broken into small pieces

12 chocolate-covered almonds

white chocolate trifle with morello cherries

SERVES 8 • PREP 15 MINS, PLUS CHILLING • COOK 5 MINS • CALS PER PORTION 510 • FAT PER PORTION 29 G

1 Layer the biscuits in the bottom of a large glass trifle dish. Mix together the juice from the morello cherries and the kirsch, and pour over the biscuits. Add the cherries and set aside.
2 Put the white chocolate pieces in a heatproof bowl, set it over a saucepan of simmering water and stir until melted. Leave to cool slightly, then fold it into the fresh custard. Cover the fruit with the custard mixture and then top with the cream. Put in the fridge to chill for 1 hour. Serve dusted with cocoa powder.

Tip
Langue de chat biscuits are long, thin, dry and slightly sweet. They are available in major supermarkets.

3 x 100 g (3½ oz) packets langue de chat biscuits

680 g (approx 1½ lb) jar morello cherries, drained and half the juice reserved

150 ml (¼ pint) kirsch

100 g (3½ oz) bar white chocolate, broken into pieces

400 g (14 oz) carton fresh custard

284 ml (approx ½ pint) carton double cream, lightly whipped

cocoa powder, for dusting

victoria sandwich

SERVES 8 • PREP 10 MINS • COOK 30 MINS • CALS PER PORTION 195 • FAT PER PORTION 10 G

1 Preheat the oven to gas mark 5/190°C (375°F). In a large bowl, whisk the eggs lightly. Add the caster sugar and whisk until thick and creamy. Using a metal spoon, fold in the sieved flour.
2 Pour the mixture into a greased 18 cm (7 in) round cake tin and bake for 30 minutes or until cooked. Check by inserting a skewer into the centre of the cake; if it comes out clean, it is ready.
3 When cool, slice the cake in half horizontally and spread with the jam and cream. Dust the top with icing sugar and serve.

2 eggs

75 g (3 oz) caster sugar

75 g (3 oz) self-raising flour

4 tablespoons raspberry jam

150 ml (¼ pint) double cream, lightly whipped

sieved icing sugar, for dusting

black forest pie

SERVES 8 • PREP 30 MINS, PLUS DEFROSTING AND CHILLING • COOK 40–45 MINS • CALS PER PORTION 455 • FAT PER PORTION 26 G

1 Defrost the frozen fruit in a sieve set over a bowl. Meanwhile, roll out one packet of the pastry on a lightly floured surface and use it to line a shallow 20.5 cm (8 in) round pie dish, 2.5 cm (1 in) deep. Trim the sides with a blunt knife and chill for 30 minutes.
2 When the fruit is defrosted, reserve 3 tablespoons of the juice collected in the bowl. Put the rest of the juice in a heavy-based pan, add the caster sugar and vanilla, and heat gently until the sugar has dissolved.
3 Mix the cornflour in a cup with the reserved juice until smooth, then add it to the sugar syrup in the pan. Stir well, then add the drained fruit. Cook gently for 5 minutes until the mixture thickens. Remove the pan from the heat, transfer its contents into a bowl and set aside to cool.
4 Preheat the oven to gas mark 6/200°C (400°F). Roll out the remaining pastry on a floured surface to a circle slightly larger than the pie dish. Spoon the cooled fruit into the pastry-lined dish, piling it slightly in middle.
5 Brush the lip of the dish with milk, then top with the pastry lid, pressing it around the lip of the dish to seal. Trim the edges and crimp using your index finger and thumb. Brush with milk and sprinkle sugar over the top.
6 Place the pie on a baking tray and bake for 40–45 minutes. Leave to stand for 15 minutes before serving.

2 x 500 g (1 lb 2 oz) packets frozen Black Forest fruits

2 x 375 g (13 oz) packets dessert shortcrust pastry, chilled

125 g (4 oz) caster sugar

½ teaspoon vanilla extract

3 teaspoons cornflour

milk, for brushing

1 teaspoon granulated sugar

new england cheesecake

SERVES 12 • PREP 30 MINS, PLUS STANDING AND CHILLING • COOK 1¼ HRS • CALS PER PORTION 690 •
FAT PER PORTION 54 G

300 g (11 oz) digestive biscuits

150 g (5 oz) butter, melted

4 x 200 g (7 oz) packets cream cheese

225 g (8 oz) caster sugar

142 ml (approx ¼ pint) carton soured cream

1 teaspoon vanilla extract

2 tablespoons cornflour

4 eggs, beaten

6 tablespoons shop-bought banoffee sauce

1 Preheat the oven to gas mark 3/160°C (325°F).

2 Whizz the biscuits in a food processor or place them in a plastic bag and crush with a rolling pin. Tip into a bowl, add the melted butter and stir well to coat. Spoon into a 20.5 cm (8 in) round springform tin and press firmly to make a base 1 cm (½ in) thick. Place in the oven and bake for 10 minutes, then allow to cool slightly. Increase the oven temperature to gas mark 4/180°C (350°F).

3 Meanwhile, in a large bowl, whisk together the cream cheese, caster sugar, soured cream, vanilla extract and cornflour until smooth. Gradually add the eggs, a little at a time, and pour the mixture over the biscuit base.

4 Beat the banoffee sauce to loosen, then add it to the cream cheese mixture and swirl the two together with a skewer.

5 Line the outside of the cake tin with strong foil so that it covers the bottom and sides in one large piece. Repeat with another layer of foil and then place it in a roasting tin. Pour hot water into the roasting tin to halfway up the sides of the cake tin. Bake in the oven for 1¼ hours until browned and firm. Turn off the oven and leave the cheesecake there for 15–20 minutes more.

6 Remove the cheesecake from the oven. Unwrap the foil and alow the cheesecake to cool. Refrigerate for 3 hours. Remove it from the fridge 20 minutes before serving.

lemon and ricotta cheesecake

SERVES 6 • PREP 20 MINS, PLUS CHILLING • COOK 40–45 MINS • CALS PER PORTION 683 • FAT PER PORTION 44 G

1 Preheat the oven to gas mark 5/190°C (375°F) and grease a shallow 20.5 cm (8 in) round, loose-bottomed tin.

2 Roll out the pastry on a lightly floured surface, and use it to carefully line the base and sides of the tin. Trim the edges and chill for about 1 hour. Prick the pastry base with a fork, place greaseproof paper on top, with its edges overlapping, and fill the pastry case with baking beans or dried peas to weight it down. Bake in the oven for 10 minutes until lightly golden.

3 Remove the baking beans and greaseproof paper and allow the pastry case to cool. Reduce the oven temperature to gas mark 3/160°C (325°F). In a large bowl, whisk the ricotta cheese, mascarpone and caster sugar until smooth. Add the lemon juice, zest and eggs and mix well.

4 Spoon the lemon cheese mixture into the pastry case, level the surface and place it in the oven. Bake for 40–45 minutes until golden. Leave the cheesecake in the tin until cool. Serve, with hot lemon curd or double cream if desired.

375 g (13 oz) packet dessert shortcrust pastry

250 g (9 oz) each of ricotta cheese and mascarpone

75 g (3 oz) caster sugar

grated zest and juice of 3 lemons

2 eggs

coffee and walnut cake

SERVES 12 • PREP 30 MINS • COOK 1 HR 10 MINS • CALS PER SLICE 618 • FAT PER SLICE 41 G

1 Preheat the oven to gas mark 4/180°C (350°F). Grease and flour a 23 cm (9 in) ring mould tin, 7.5 cm (3 in) deep.
2 In a large bowl, cream the butter and sugar until light and fluffy. Gradually add the beaten eggs, a little at a time, whisking well after each addition. Using a large metal spoon, fold in the sifted flour and the walnuts. Stir in the cooled coffee solution.
3 Spoon the mixture into the prepared ring mould and level it out using the back of a spoon. Place in the oven and bake for 1 hour 10 minutes until risen. The cake is ready when it springs back when pressed lightly with the fingertips and when a skewer inserted in the centre comes out clean. Allow the cake to cool in the tin before serving.

350 g (12 oz) butter, softened

350 g (12 oz) light brown sugar

6 medium eggs, beaten

350 g (12 oz) self-raising flour, sifted

250 g (9 oz) walnuts, chopped

3 teaspoons instant coffee dissolved in 3 tablespoons boiling water, cooled

orange and buttercream cake

SERVES 8 • PREP 20 MINS • COOK NONE • CALS PER SLICE 790 • FAT PER SLICE 46 G

2 sweet flan cases

100 g (3½ oz) plain chocolate

5 oranges, peeled and sliced

For the buttercream:

500 g (1 lb 2 oz) icing sugar

350 g (12 oz) butter

2 tablespoons Grand Marnier
or orange juice

1 Using a sharp knife, remove the outer edge of both flan rings to leave two sponge cakes.
2 Grate half the chocolate and shape the rest into decorative curls using a vegetable peeler.
3 To make the buttercream, fold the icing sugar into the butter until the mixture is pale and creamy. Beat in the Grand Marnier or orange juice, adding a little water if the mixture is too stiff.
4 Spread half the buttercream on one sponge base and sprinkle with the grated chocolate, then sandwich the two cakes together.
5 Cover the top and sides of the cake with the remaining buttercream, then top with the orange slices. Scatter the chocolate curls on top.

iced garland cake

MAKES 24 SLICES • PREP 20 MINS, PLUS DECORATING • COOK 2–2¼ HRS • CALS PER SLICE 480 • FAT PER SLICE 18 G

1 Preheat the oven to gas mark 2/150°C (300°F). Grease and line a 20 cm (7¾ in) round cake tin. Mix together the dried fruits and nuts.
2 In another bowl cream the butter and sugar together until light and fluffy. Gradually add the eggs, beating well after each addition. If necessary, add a little of the flour to prevent curdling.
3 Sift the flour and spices into the bowl and fold in using a metal spoon. Fold in the almonds, fruits and nuts until evenly combined.
4 Turn the mixture into the cake tin and level the surface. Bake for 2–2¼ hours or until just firm and a skewer inserted into the centre comes out clean. Leave to cool in the tin, then wrap well in greaseproof paper and foil and store in a cool place for up to a month before decorating.
5 To decorate the cake, invert it onto a 25.5 cm (10 in) round cake board. Press a little almond paste, warmed in your hands, around the base of the cake to fill the gap between the cake and the board.
6 Melt the apricot jam in a saucepan with 1 tablespoon water, then press through a sieve. Brush over the top and sides of the cake.
7 Roll out the remaining almond paste on a surface dusted with icing sugar to a 29 cm (11 in) round. Lift the paste over the cake and ease it to fit around the sides. Trim off the excess around the base.
8 Lightly beat the egg whites in a large bowl. Gradually whisk in the icing sugar to make smooth, softly peaking icing. Spoon up a little icing so that it falls to an icicle-like point from the spoon; if it doesn't, work in a tiny amount of cold water. Touch the top edge of the cake with the back of the spoon so the icing hangs down the side like an icicle. Repeat all around the cake, making the icicles various lengths. Swirl the remaining icing onto the top of the cake, lightly peaking it with the back of the spoon or a palette knife.
9 Dust the rosemary sprigs with plenty of icing sugar and arrange them around the top edges of the cake. Scatter the silver-coated almonds around them. Crush the mints while still in their wrappers, then unwrap and scatter the pieces around the other decorations.
10 Lightly dust with icing sugar, then decorate the base of the cake and the board with cord and ribbon.

Tip
You may prefer to ice the cake up to two weeks in advance and add the decorations later, as these will deteriorate in a few days.

150 g (5 oz) no-soak dried apricots, roughly chopped

100 g (3½ oz) glacé cherries, halved

125 g (4 oz) dried mango or pears, roughly chopped

350 g (12 oz) sultanas

100 g (3½ oz) brazil nuts or almonds, roughly chopped

300 g (11 oz) unsalted butter

300 g (11 oz) caster sugar

5 eggs

300 g (11 oz) plain flour

1 teaspoon each ground mixed spice and cinnamon

75 g (3 oz) ground almonds

For the decoration:

750 g (1 lb 10 oz) white almond paste

3 tablespoons apricot jam

700 g (1½ lb) icing sugar, plus extra for dusting

3 egg whites

sprigs of fresh rosemary

1 handful each silver-coated sugared almonds and wrapped clear boiled mints

silver cord and ribbon

portable feasts

From lavish picnics to lunchbox sandwiches, portable food must be easy to wrap, carry and eat – but that doesn't mean it has to be boring! The ideas here will add interest to meals on the move. Buying take-out lunches every day is expensive and usually the food is high in fat and salt. By preparing your own, you will be looking after your health and your purse, too.

gazpacho

SERVES 8 • PREP 40 MINS • COOK NONE • CALS PER PORTION 150 • FAT PER PORTION 6 G

1 In a large bowl, put the onion, peppers, cucumber, garlic, celery and chilli, and stir well. Mix in the tomato purée and canned tomatoes.

2 Transfer half the mixture to a blender, add the tomato juice and 300 ml (½ pint) water and whizz until smooth. Pour into the bowl with the rest of the tomato mixture. Season well with salt and black pepper and put into the fridge to chill until required.

3 To make the croûtons, heat the olive oil in a frying pan until hot. Add the bread and fry until crispy and golden. Drain on absorbent kitchen paper.

4 When ready to serve, add the croûtons to the soup and sprinkle chopped parsley over the top, to garnish.

1 red onion, diced

2 red peppers, cored, deseeded and diced

½ cucumber, diced

4 garlic cloves, crushed

2 celery sticks, diced

1 large red chilli, deseeded and finely chopped

2–3 tablespoons tomato purée

2 x 400 g (14 oz) cans chopped tomatoes

300 ml (½ pint) tomato juice

3 tablespoons chopped fresh flat leaf parsley, to garnish

For the croûtons:

3 tablespoons olive oil

6–8 slices of ciabatta bread, cut into cubes

caponata

SERVES 4 • PREP 15 MINS • COOK 20 MINS • CALS PER PORTION 163 • FAT PER PORTION 14 G

1 In a large frying pan, heat half the oil, add the garlic and cook for 30 seconds until golden. Add the celery, cook for 2 minutes, then add the tomatoes. Simmer gently for 10 minutes, or until most of the liquid has evaporated.
2 Heat the remaining oil in another pan and cook the aubergine for 5–6 minutes, or until slightly browned.
3 Stir the aubergines, pinenuts and capers into the tomatoes. Season with salt and pepper. Allow to cool slightly, stir in the parsley and refrigerate.

2 tablespoons olive oil

2 garlic cloves, crushed

2 celery sticks, sliced

400 g (14 oz) can chopped tomatoes

1 large aubergine, cut into 2.5 cm (1 in) cubes

50 g (2 oz) pinenuts

1 tablespoon capers

1 bunch of parsley, chopped

goats' cheese and red pepper tart

SERVES 4 • PREP 25 MINS, PLUS CHILLING • COOK 50 MINS • CALS PER PORTION 470 • FAT PER PORTION 33 G

1 Preheat the oven to gas mark 6/ 200°C (400°F). Grease a 20.5 cm (8 in) flan tin and line it with pastry. Prick the base and chill for 20 minutes.
2 Cover with greaseproof paper, fill with rice or baking beans and bake for 10 minutes, discard and bake for another 10 minutes. Reduce the oven to gas mark 5/190°C (375°F).
3 Heat the oil in a saucepan and cook the peppers for 5 minutes. Stir in the thyme, spoon onto the pastry and add the olives and goat's cheese.
4 Beat the eggs and cream. Season with salt and pepper and pour onto the tart. Bake for 20–25 minutes.

225 g (8 oz) packet ready-rolled shortcrust pastry

1 tablespoon olive oil

2 large red peppers, chopped

2 tablespoons chopped thyme

12 pitted black olives

100 g (3½ oz) goats' cheese, crumbled

2 medium eggs

150 ml (¼ pint) single cream

portable tomato mozzarella salad

SERVES 4–6 • PREP 10 MINS • COOK NONE • CALS PER PORTION 675–450 • FAT PER PORTION 60–40 G

10 ripe tomatoes, sliced

1 handful of basil leaves (optional)

3 x 150 g (5 oz) packets fresh mozzarella, sliced

200 ml (7 fl oz) olive oil

juice of 1 lemon

1 Layer the tomatoes, basil and mozzarella, in a large kilner jar, seasoning the layers with freshly ground black pepper as you work.
2 Mix together the olive oil and lemon juice and carefully pour over the top of the salad.
3 To serve, add salt to taste.

Variations

To add extra flavours to this simple salad, try adding slices of chargrilled courgette or aubergine, or stirring pesto into the olive oil.

spicy bean salad

SERVES 10 • PREP 10 MINS • COOK NONE • CALS PER PORTION 140 • FAT PER PORTION 1 G

4 x 410 g (approx 14 oz) cans mixed pulses, drained and rinsed

3 garlic cloves, crushed

1 bird's eye red chilli, finely chopped

1 green pepper, cored, deseeded and finely chopped

pinch of cumin seeds

grated zest and juice of 1 orange

1 bunch of flat leaf parsley, roughly chopped

1 Put the canned pulses in a large bowl. Add the garlic, chilli, green pepper and cumin seeds, and mix well.
2 Stir in the orange juice and zest. Add the chopped parsley just before serving.

crab mayonnaise on sourdough bread

SERVES 4 • PREP 10 MINS • COOK NONE • CALS PER PORTION 350 • FAT PER PORTION 19 G

2 x 170 g (approx 6 oz) cans crabmeat

2 tablespoons mayonnaise

2 pinches of paprika

8 slices of sourdough loaf

8 slices of gherkin

100 g (3½ oz) packet salad leaves

1 Drain the crabmeat, place in a small mixing bowl and flake it well with a fork.

2 Add 1 tablespoon of the mayonnaise and a pinch of paprika to the crabmeat and mix well.

3 Lay out four slices of the sourdough bread and top each with two slices of gherkin. Divide the crabmeat mayonnaise among the sandwiches and top each one with salad leaves and a little mayonnaise.

4 Sprinkle each sandwich with a little of the remaining paprika and some freshly ground black pepper. Top each slice with the remaining bread, sandwich together and serve immediately.

triple-decker mushroom sandwiches
with chilli chutney

SERVES 4 • PREP 15 MINS • COOK 2 MINS • CALS PER PORTION 360 • FAT PER PORTION 20 G

1 Place the tomato and mushroom slices on a baking tray and cook under a preheated grill for 2 minutes.

2 To assemble the sandwiches, lay out four slices of herbed bread and top them with half of the mushrooms, tomatoes and cheese. Next, smother each one with half the chilli jelly then top with another slice of bread.

3 Make a second layer by adding the remaining tomatoes, mushrooms, cheese and chilli jelly. Stack the final slice of bread on top and press each sandwich together firmly.

2 large tomatoes, sliced

125 g (4 oz) large mushrooms, sliced

12 slices of herbed bread

225 g (8 oz) Monterey jack cheese, sliced

10 teaspoons chilli jelly

mediterranean club sandwiches

MAKES 10 • PREP 10 MINS • COOK NONE • CALS PER SANDWICH 230 • FAT PER SANDWICH 10 G

5 focaccia rolls

135 g (approx 4½ oz) jar tapenade

2 x 150 g (5 oz) packets mozzarella balls, sliced

250 g (9 oz) cherry tomatoes, sliced

50 g (2 oz) packet rocket leaves

1 Slice the focaccia rolls in half and then half again.
2 Spread half of the slices with a little tapenade. Then top with slices of mozzarella, sliced tomatoes and rocket leaves. Season well with ground black pepper.
3 Place a focaccia half on top of each sandwich and secure with a wooden cocktail stick.

Variations

Tapenade is an olive paste available from delis and most supermarkets, but if you cannot find it, replace it with chopped pitted olives. Sliced ciabatta is an alternative to focaccia bread.

spicy sausage with mixed peppers
on toasted baguette

SERVES 4 • PREP 15 MINS • COOK 25 MINS • CALS PER PORTION 400 • FAT PER PORTION 14 G

1 Preheat the oven to gas mark 7/220°C (425°F).
2 Put the peppers in a roasting tin and drizzle with 1 tablespoon of the olive oil, using your fingers to coat them well. Roast the peppers for 15 minutes, until their skins start to shrivel slightly.
3 Remove the peppers from the oven and leave to cool until they can be handled. Remove the skins, then halve, deseed and slice the peppers into strips.
4 Heat the remaining oil in a frying pan. When hot, add the peppers and cook for 2–3 minutes, then add the white wine vinegar and stir. Leave to cook for 5 minutes until the pepper mixture begins to thicken, then stir in the brown sugar and cook for a further 2 minutes.
5 Meanwhile, toast the baguette halves. Cover four halves with slices of sausage. Use a slotted spoon to remove the peppers from the pan and place them on top of the sausage. Top each baguette with the remaining baguette halves.

1 green pepper

1 red pepper

1 yellow pepper

2 tablespoons olive oil

1 tablespoon white wine vinegar

1 tablespoon brown sugar

2 baguettes, halved then sliced in half lengthways

16 slices of spicy sausage

fiery steak sandwiches

SERVES 4 • PREP 15 MINS • COOK 16 MINS • CALS PER PORTION 540 • FAT PER PORTION 27 G

1 Make the horseradish butter. Mix the butter and horseradish sauce together until well combined then shape into a block. Wrap the butter in clear film and refrigerate until required.
2 Preheat the oven to gas mark 7/220°C (425°F). Put the onion in a roasting tin and drizzle with 1 tablespoon of the olive oil. Cook for 10 minutes until slightly charred. Remove and set aside.
3 Heat the remaining olive oil in a frying pan. Add two steaks and cook for 3 minutes, then turn over and cook for a further 3 minutes. Keep them warm while you cook the other two steaks.
4 Meanwhile, split the ciabattas in half and toast them under a preheated grill. To assemble, lay a steak on one half of each roll and top with the horseradish butter and fried onion. Sprinkle with ground black pepper and garnish with tarragon sprigs. Sandwich together.

50 g (2 oz) soft butter

2 teaspoons horseradish sauce

1 large onion, roughly chopped

2 tablespoons olive oil

4 ciabatta rolls

4 x 175 g (6 oz) sirloin steaks

8 sprigs of fresh tarragon

chilli falafel pittas with herbed yogurt

SERVES 4 • PREP 20 MINS • COOK 15 MINS • CALS PER PORTION 400 • FAT PER PORTION 14 G

1 Make up the falafel mixture according to packet instructions. Shape into eight patties and fry them in the sunflower oil, again according to packet instructions.

2 To make the herbed yogurt, stir the chopped parsley into the yogurt and season with ground black pepper.

3 Warm the pitta breads under a preheated grill. Slice one long side off each pitta to make pockets and fill each pocket with two falafel, sliced chilli and yogurt to serve.

Tip

These falafel-filled pitta pockets can be served cold or warm – they are great to munch on a hot day in the garden. Omit the chillies and the kids will love them, too.

284 g (10½ oz) packet falafel mix

4 tablespoons sunflower oil

2 tablespoons chopped fresh parsley

150 g (5 oz) tub plain yogurt

4 pitta breads

1 large red chilli, thinly sliced

spinach and feta filo rolls

MAKES 6 • PREP 20 MINS • COOK 40 MINS • CALS PER ROLL 345 • FAT PER ROLL 28 G

1 Heat 1 tablespoon of the butter in a large saucepan. Add the spinach to the pan. Stir well, cover and cook for about 2 minutes or until wilted. Tip the spinach into a colander, rinse with cold water and squeeze all the liquid out. Chop roughly.

2 In a bowl, mix the spinach, dill or fennel seeds, crumbled feta cheese and egg yolks. Mix very well. Season with a little salt and plenty of ground black pepper.

3 Preheat the oven to gas mark 4/180°C (350°F). Lay out a sheet of filo and brush with melted butter. Place another sheet of filo on top. Cut the layered sheets in half. Repeat with the remaining sheets – two per layer, so you have six pieces when cut. Brush each piece with melted butter.

4 Divide the spinach mixture among the six pieces. Fold in the edges of the pastry and roll up to make tube shapes. Brush the filo rolls with the remaining butter and sprinkle with a mixture of sesame and mustard seeds.

5 Place the filo rolls on a lightly greased baking tray and bake for 40 minutes or until light brown and crisp. Cool on a wire rack. Serve as part of an elegant picnic or in a lunchbox.

50 g (2 oz) butter, melted

225 g (8 oz) young spinach leaves, trimmed and stalks removed

1 teaspoon dill or fennel seeds

200 g (7 oz) packet feta cheese, crumbled

2 egg yolks

6 large sheets of filo pastry

1 tablespoon sesame seeds

1 tablespoon mustard seeds

sticky soy and coriander chicken

SERVES 8 • PREP 5 MINS, PLUS MARINATING • COOK 45 MINS • CALS PER PORTION 315 • FAT PER PORTION 12 G

1 Place the chicken pieces in a shallow dish. Mix all the marinade ingredients together and pour over the chicken. Stir well to coat the chicken and leave to marinate overnight.
2 Preheat the oven to gas mark 6/200°C (400°F). Place the chicken pieces in a roasting tin or ovenproof dish and bake for 45 minutes until cooked through. Remove and cool.
3 Toss with the chopped fresh coriander to serve. Coleslaw makes an ideal accompaniment to the chicken.

8 chicken pieces, such as thighs, wings and drumsticks

2 tablespoons chopped fresh coriander

For the marinade:

4 tablespoons soft brown sugar

2 tablespoons sesame oil

1 tablespoon lime or lemon juice or vinegar

½ teaspoon ground coriander

4 tablespoons soy sauce

cornish pasties

MAKES 6 LARGE PASTIES • PREP 25 MINS • COOK 1 HR • CALS PER PASTY 1200 • FAT PER PASTY 80 G

2 tablespoons sunflower oil

375 g (13 oz) potatoes, peeled and diced

275 g (10 oz) carrots, peeled and diced

2 onions, chopped

450 g (1 lb) minced beef

150 g (5 oz) mushrooms, finely chopped

1 teaspoon tomato paste

3 x 500 g (1 lb 2 oz) packets puff or shortcrust pastry

3 tablespoons milk

1 Heat the oil gently in a large pan. Add the potatoes, carrots and onions, stir and cook, covered, over a gentle heat for 15 minutes.
2 In a large frying pan, fry the minced beef in batches until brown. Add to the potato mixture with the mushrooms, tomato paste and 150 ml (¼ pint) water. Season well with salt and ground black pepper and simmer gently for 30 minutes until no liquid remains. Allow to cool.
3 Preheat the oven to gas mark 6/200°C (400°F). Roll out the pastry in batches on a lightly floured surface. Cut out two large circles, 20.5 cm (8 in) in diameter, from each packet of pastry using an upturned bowl. Divide the cooled filling among the six pastry rounds, placing it in the middle of the pastry.
4 Brush the edges of each pastry round with milk, then fold over to form a pasty. Pinch the edges together well to seal the pasties, brush their tops with milk and place on a lightly greased baking tray. Place in the oven and bake for 25 minutes or until golden. Remove the pasties from the baking tray and leave to cool on wire racks.

chocolate brownie nests

MAKES 12 • PREP 10 MINS • COOK 20 MINS • CALS PER PORTION 470 • FAT PER PORTION 27 G

1 Preheat the oven to gas mark 4/180°C (350°F). Line a muffin tin with 12 muffin cases.

2 Put the chocolate and the butter in a heatproof bowl over a pan of barely simmering water, making sure the water does not touch the bowl. Gently heat until melted.

3 In a large bowl, mix the flour, sugar, eggs and chocolate chunks. Add the melted chocolate and stir until combined. Spoon into muffin cases until half full. Bake in the oven for 20 minutes until risen. Allow to cool completely on a wire rack.

4 To decorate, spread each muffin with chocolate spread. Crumble the chocolate flakes into small chunks and place on top, like a 'nest'. Divide the marzipan into three and dye each a different colour. Roll each third into 12 small eggs and top each muffin with 3 different-coloured eggs.

65 g (2¾ oz) plain chocolate (minimum 70 per cent cocoa solids)

160 g (5½ oz) unsalted butter

100 g (3½ oz) self-raising flour, sieved

200 g (7 oz) caster sugar

3 medium eggs, beaten

125 g (4 oz) plain chocolate chunks

To decorate:

8 tablespoons chocolate spread

3 chocolate flakes

225 g (8 oz) natural marzipan

3 colours of food dye

strawberry and cream wraps

MAKES 6 • PREP 15 MINS • COOK NONE • CALS PER WRAP 360 • FAT PER WRAP 27 G

1 Lay the pancakes out flat and divide the sliced strawberries among them. Bring the two edges of each pancake into the middle to enclose the strawberries and wrap the pancakes in greaseproof paper.
2 Lightly whip the double cream, mix in the icing sugar and store the whipped cream in a container, ready to travel.
3 To serve, place a spoonful of cream on top of each pancake.

1 packet of 6 ready-made sweet pancakes

18 strawberries, about 250 g (9 oz), sliced

250 ml (8 fl oz) double cream

1 teaspoon icing sugar

busy parents and healthy kids

Feeding children, especially after a long day at work, can
be a real challenge – especially as they can be fussy eaters.
Here you will find imaginative recipes that will, hopefully,
encourage your children to eat more healthy foods. Investing
in a child's diet is important, as it will have a massive
impact on their health as they grow older.

easy tomato-veggie soup
with cheese toasts

SERVES 4 • PREP 15 MINS • COOK 30 MINS • CALS PER PORTION 316 • FAT PER PORTION 18 G

1 Heat the olive oil in a large saucepan then add the onion, carrot and celery. Cook over a very low heat with the lid on for 20 minutes. Add the tomatoes, garlic and thyme, stir well and simmer for 5 minutes.

2 Add the vegetable stock, bring to the boil, then simmer for 5 minutes and remove from the heat. Whizz in a blender to a smooth consistency. Season with salt and black pepper to taste.

3 To make the toasts, preheat the oven to gas mark 6/200°C (400°F). Cut each slice of bread into four or five pieces. Place on a baking tray and bake for 10 minutes. Top each piece with grated cheese and return to the oven for about 3 minutes until melted. Serve hot with the soup.

3 tablespoons olive oil

1 red onion, chopped

1 carrot, peeled and chopped

2 celery sticks, chopped

700 g (1½ lb) tomatoes, chopped

½ garlic clove, crushed

1 teaspoon dried thyme

450 ml (¾ pint) vegetable stock

For the toasts:

4 slices of bread, such as tomato focaccia

50 g (2 oz) cheese, grated

vegetable stick salad with hummus

SERVES 4 • PREP 15 MINS • COOK NONE • CALS PER PORTION 165 • FAT PER PORTION 8 G

½ cucumber

3 large carrots, peeled, or
150 g (5 oz) baby carrots

1 courgette

1 red pepper, cored, deseeded
and cut into strips

1 yellow pepper, cored,
deseeded and cut into strips

1 bunch of radishes

175 g (6 oz) tub hummus or
your favourite dip

1 Cut the cucumber in half lengthways and scrape out the seeds.
Cut into sticks.
2 Cut the carrots and courgette into sticks.
3 Arrange all the vegetables on individual plates and spoon the
hummus or other chosen dip into the centre for dipping.

sweetcorn and pesto pizzas

SERVES 4 • PREP 10 MINS • COOK 20 MINS • CALS PER PORTION 350 • FAT PER PORTION 16 G

1 Preheat the oven to gas mark 6/200°C (400°F). Slice the ciabatta in half lengthways, and then slice into four pieces. Place the bread on a baking tray and cook for 5 minutes.
2 Spread each slice of bread with about 1 tablespoon pesto. Sprinkle over 1 tablespoon sweetcorn, top with slices of mozzarella and sprinkle with more sweetcorn. Season with salt and ground black pepper, drizzle with a little oil and bake for 15 minutes.

½ ciabatta bread loaf

190 g (6¾ oz) jar red pesto

200 g (7 oz) can sweetcorn

150 g (5 oz) packet fresh mozzarella, sliced

olive oil, for drizzling

penne with chunky peppers

SERVES 4 • PREP 10 MINS • COOK 15–20 MINS • CALS PER PORTION 444 • FAT PER PORTION 3 G

3 large mixed peppers, cored, deseeded and cut into squares

1 chilli, chopped

2 garlic cloves, crushed

350 ml (12 fl oz) vegetable stock

450 g (1 lb) dried penne

fresh basil leaves, to serve

1 Mix together the peppers, freshly chopped chilli and garlic. Add to a frying pan with the vegetable stock and simmer until tender and the sauce is syrupy.

2 Meanwhile cook the pasta in a large saucepan of boiling, salted water, according to packet instructions.

3 Drain the pasta, mix with the sauce and sprinkle with basil.

vegetable gang lasagne

SERVES 4 • PREP 20 MINS • COOK 1 HR • CALS PER PORTION 425 • FAT PER PORTION 23 G

1 Preheat the oven to gas mark 6/200°C (400°F). Put all the vegetables and garlic on a baking tray and drizzle with the oil.
2 Place in the oven and roast for 20 minutes, until slightly charred. Leave to cool, then remove the skins from the pepper, cut it in half, deseed and slice. Remove the skins from the garlic cloves. Then mix all the roasted vegetables with the canned chopped tomatoes. Season well with salt and black pepper.
3 To assemble the lasagne, put one-third of the vegetable and tomato mixture into a large ovenproof dish. Sprinkle with half the basil, then top with half the lasagne sheets and half of the ricotta cheese. Repeat the layers, finishing with a layer of the vegetable and tomato mixture.
4 Cover the assembled lasagne with slices of mozzarella and bake for 40 minutes. Serve hot, with a mixed salad drizzled with a fruity dressing if desired.

Tip
Using ricotta cheese instead of cheese sauce in this lasagne cuts down on preparation time and is a healthier option, too, as the ricotta is lower in fat.

1 red pepper

2 courgettes, roughly chopped

1 aubergine, roughly chopped

1 red onion, roughly chopped

2 garlic cloves, unpeeled

1 tablespoon olive oil

400 g (14 oz) can chopped tomatoes

1 handful of basil leaves, torn

10 sheets of no-cook lasagne

450 g (1 lb) ricotta cheese

125 g (4 oz) mozzarella, sliced

spaghetti bolognese

SERVES 4 • PREP 10 MINS • COOK 50 MINS • CALS PER PORTION 595 • FAT PER PORTION 14 G

75 g (3 oz) unsmoked bacon, diced

2 tablespoons olive oil

225 g (8 oz) lean minced beef

1 medium onion, chopped

1 celery stick, chopped

1 garlic clove, crushed

125 g (4 oz) mushrooms, sliced

300 ml (½ pint) chicken stock

225 g (8 oz) can chopped tomatoes

1 teaspoon tomato purée

400 g (14 oz) dried spaghetti

1 In a medium-sized saucepan, fry the bacon in its own fat until lightly browned. Remove from the pan and set aside. Add 1 tablespoon of the oil and fry the mince until well browned. Remove from the pan and set aside.

2 Add the remaining oil and cook the onions and celery over a low heat, stirring occasionally, until soft and lightly coloured. Add the garlic and mushrooms and cook for a further 1 minute.

3 Return the minced beef and bacon to the saucepan, stir in the stock, tomatoes and tomato purée and season with salt and ground black pepper. Bring to the boil, then cover and simmer for 45 minutes.

4 Meanwhile, cook the spaghetti in a large saucepan of boiling, salted water, according to packet instructions. Drain well.

5 Serve the cooked pasta and bolognese sauce with grated Parmesan and a green salad if desired.

sticky ribs

SERVES 4 • PREP 5 MINS, PLUS MARINATING • COOK 1½ HRS • CALS PER PORTION 155 • FAT PER PORTION 4 G

1 Thoroughly mix all the marinade ingredients together in a small glass bowl. Place the ribs in a non-stick baking tray and pour the marinade over them, then turn them to make sure they are evenly coated.

2 Leave to marinate for at least 1 hour, but preferably overnight if possible, as this will impart more flavour to the meat.

3 Preheat the oven to gas mark 3/160°C (325°F). Bake the ribs for about 1½ hours.

4 Check the ribs after 40 minutes and turn them. You may need to add a little water if the marinade is catching to the pan. Serve the ribs hot or cold.

700 g (1½ lb) pork ribs

For the marinade:

3 tablespoons Worcestershire sauce

3 tablespoons dark soy sauce

2 tablespoons prepared English mustard

150 ml (¼ pint) tomato ketchup

3 tablespoons honey

cheese and onion burgers

SERVES 4 • PREP 15 MINS • COOK 10 MINS • CALS PER BURGER 470 • FAT PER BURGER 20 G

1 egg, beaten

150 g (5 oz) fresh white breadcrumbs

125 g (4 oz) cheddar, grated

½ onion, finely diced

1 teaspoon roughly chopped fresh sage

½ teaspoon Dijon mustard

2 tablespoons olive oil

To assemble:

4 bread rolls, lightly toasted

100 g (3 oz) packet mixed salad leaves

½ red onion, thinly sliced

4 teaspoons relish (optional)

Tip
These burgers can be cooked ahead and frozen – microwave them when required.

1 In a large bowl, mix half of the beaten egg with 75 g (3 oz) of the breadcrumbs, the grated cheese, onion, sage and mustard. Divide the mixture into four. If the mixture is too wet, add more breadcrumbs. Shape the four portions into burgers.
2 Brush each burger with the remaining beaten egg and coat with the remaining breadcrumbs.
3 Heat the olive oil in a large frying pan, add the burgers and fry for 4–5 minutes on each side until golden.
4 To serve, put the burgers in the lightly toasted bread rolls, top with salad leaves, sliced onion and a generous dollop of your favourite sauce or relish.

sticky chicken pieces and couscous

SERVES 4 • PREP 5 MINS • COOK 20–25 MINS • CALS PER PORTION 300 • FAT PER PORTION 5 G

2 tablespoons honey

1 teaspoon soy sauce

4 chicken thighs, approx
500 g (1 lb 2 oz) total weight

2 tablespoons sesame seeds

For the couscous:

300 g (11 oz) couscous

500 ml (17 fl oz) vegetable stock

1 red pepper, cored, deseeded
and finely chopped

3 tablespoons chopped fresh
flat leaf parsley

1 Preheat the oven to gas mark 6/200°C (400°F).

2 Mix together the honey and soy sauce. Place the chicken thighs in a roasting tin. Coat with the honey and soy sauce, then sprinkle with the sesame seeds.

3 Place in the oven and cook for 20–25 minutes until the chicken thighs are cooked through.

4 Meanwhile, prepare the couscous. Tip the couscous into a heatproof bowl and pour in the vegetable stock. Stir with a fork, cover with a clean tea towel and leave for 10 minutes. Fluff up with a fork, stir in the pepper and parsley and season well with salt and ground black pepper. Serve with the sticky chicken.

turkey escalopes with ham

SERVES 4 • PREP 20 MINS • COOK 15–20 MINS • CALS PER PORTION 360 • FAT PER PORTION 17 G

4 x 125 g (4 oz) turkey escalopes, about 1 cm (½ in) thick

4 thin slices of ham

125 g (4 oz) dried breadcrumbs

50 g (2 oz) any hard cheese, grated

1 tablespoon dried mixed herbs

4 tablespoons flour

2 eggs, beaten

1 teaspoon butter

1 tablespoon vegetable oil

lemon wedges, to serve

1 Using a sharp knife, carefully slice a pocket into each piece of turkey and place a slice of ham inside.

2 In a bowl, mix together the breadcrumbs, grated cheese and dried mixed herbs.

3 Dip each piece of turkey into the flour, coating it lightly, then dip into the beaten egg and then the breadcrumb mixture.

4 Heat the butter and oil together in a large frying pan. Fry the crumbed escalopes for about 3–4 minutes on each side until cooked through. Serve with a wedge of lemon and a green salad.

thai corn fritters

SERVES 4 • PREP 5 MINS • COOK 15 MINS • CALS PER PORTION 170 • FAT PER PORTION 6 G

50 g (2 oz) polenta

200 g (7 oz) can sweetcorn, drained

1 teaspoon chilli flakes

3 tablespoons chopped fresh coriander

1 tablespoon Thai green curry paste

1 tablespoon fish sauce

1 egg, beaten

1 tablespoon sunflower oil

1 Place the polenta in a large mixing bowl and stir in the sweetcorn, chilli flakes, coriander, green curry paste, fish sauce and beaten egg. Mix together until you have a combined sloppy mixture.

2 Heat the oil in a frying pan, then drop spoonfuls of the mixture into the pan. Cook the fritters in batches over a medium heat for 3–4 minutes each side, until cooked through and golden.

prawn biryani

SERVES 4 • PREP 10 MINS • COOK 20 MINS • CALS PER PORTION 290 • FAT PER PORTION 5 G

150 g (5 oz) long-grain rice

1 bay leaf

1 teaspoon ground turmeric

1 tablespoon olive oil

1 onion, chopped

125 g (4 oz) mushrooms, chopped

125 g (4 oz) frozen peas, cooked

150 g (5 oz) low-fat plain yogurt

225 g (8 oz) cooked peeled prawns

2 tablespoons flaked almonds (optional)

2 tablespoons sultanas (optional)

1 Put the rice, bay leaf and turmeric in a large saucepan with plenty of water. Cook for 15 minutes, or until the rice is tender.
2 Meanwhile, heat the oil in a large frying pan, add the onion and mushrooms and cook for 5 minutes. Add the peas and yogurt, and stir. Simmer for about 5 minutes, stirring occasionally. Add the prawns and cook for another 5 minutes. The mixture will curdle at first, but continue cooking until it is almost dry.
3 Drain the rice and remove the bay leaf. Serve the prawns on a bed of rice. Sprinkle with almonds and sultanas, if using.

baked potato fish pie

SERVES 4 • PREP 20 MINS • COOK 1½ HRS • CALS PER PORTION 350 • FAT PER PORTION 15 G

1 Preheat the oven to gas mark 6/200°C (400°F). Brush the potatoes with oil, season lightly with salt and bake for 1 hour or until cooked inside.

2 Towards the end of the potato cooking time, cook the cauliflower florets in a saucepan of boiling water for 3 minutes. Add the broccoli and cook for a further 1 minute. Drain the vegetables and cool with cold running water.

3 Place the fish in a wide saucepan, cover with the milk and poach gently, covered, for about 4 minutes or until just cooked. Remove the fish, reserving the milk, and gently remove its skin.

4 When the potatoes are cooked, cut a generous lid off the tops and scoop all the insides out into a large bowl. Reduce the oven temperature to gas mark 4/180°C (350°F).

5 Add enough of the reserved hot milk to the scooped-out potato to make a smooth mash. Add the flaked fish, grated cheese and the cooked vegetables. Season with a little salt and black pepper. Fold through very gently, then refill each potato skin generously. Place on a baking sheet and return to the oven for 30 minutes.

4 baking potatoes

2 tablespoons sunflower oil

200 g (7 oz) cauliflower florets

200 g (7 oz) broccoli florets

1 large smoked undyed haddock fillet, about 350 g (12 oz)

200 ml (7 fl oz) full-fat milk

125 g (4 oz) mild cheddar, grated

stuffed baked peppers

SERVES 4 • PREP 15 MINS • COOK 30 MINS • CALS PER PORTION 333 • FAT PER PORTION 16 G

1 Preheat the oven to gas mark 4/180°C (350°F). Cut a lid off the top of each pepper and scrape out the seeds.
2 Place the bulgar wheat or couscous into a large bowl, season with salt and ground black pepper and just cover with boiling water. Add the olive oil, cover and allow to stand for 5 minutes.
3 Fork through the bulgar wheat or couscous and crumble in the feta cheese. Stir in the chopped herbs.
4 Stuff each pepper generously with the mixture and bake on an oiled baking tray for about 30 minutes, with the lids to one side. Serve the stuffed baked peppers topped with the lids.

4 small red or yellow peppers

200 g (7 oz) bulgar wheat or couscous

4 tablespoons olive oil

100 g (3½ oz) feta cheese

4 tablespoons chopped soft fresh herbs, such as parsley, basil or coriander

carrot risotto

SERVES 4 • PREP 10 MINS • COOK 30 MINS • CALS PER PORTION 600 • FAT PER PORTION 26 G

1 Melt the butter in a wide saucepan. Add the chopped onion and cook gently for 5 minutes. Add the diced carrots and cook for another 5 minutes.

2 Add the rice and stir well; cook for 1 minute, stirring. Pour in enough carrot soup to just cover the rice and keep stirring. Once the liquid has been absorbed, repeat the process, adding more soup. If you run out of soup before the rice is cooked, add boiling water instead.

3 The rice should be cooked after about 20 minutes. Once it is ready, remove the pan from the heat and stir in the cheese and parsley. Season with salt and ground black pepper and serve.

50 g (2 oz) butter

1 small onion, finely chopped

200 g (7 oz) carrots, diced

300 g (11 oz) risotto rice

600 ml (1 pint) fresh carrot soup, warmed

150 g (5 oz) Parmesan, freshly grated

2 tablespoons chopped fresh parsley

cheeky chow mein

SERVES 4 • PREP 20 MINS • COOK 10 MINS • CALS PER PORTION 500 • FAT PER PORTION 16 G

1 tablespoon olive oil

450 g (1 lb) tenderloin pork, sliced lengthways into 5 cm (2 in) strips

1 red onion, sliced

2 carrots, cut into ribbons with a vegetable peeler

2 Braeburn apples, cored and sliced

½ Savoy cabbage, finely shredded

500 g (1 lb 2 oz) packet egg noodles

soy sauce, to taste

1 Heat the oil in a large frying pan over a medium heat. Add the pork strips and cook for about 5 minutes.
2 Add the onion and carrots to the pan and cook for 2 minutes. Add the apple slices and cook for a further 2 minutes, then stir in the shredded cabbage. Cook for 1 minute more, or until the vegetables are tender.
3 Meanwhile, cook the noodles according to packet instructions. When the noodles are cooked, drain then add to the pork and vegetables. Combine well, season with soy sauce and serve.

banana and toffee brûlée

SERVES 4 • PREP 10 MINS, PLUS CHILLING • COOK 1–2 MINS • CALS PER PORTION 230 • FAT PER PORTION 6 G

1 Place the digestive biscuits in a plastic bag and crush them with a rolling pin. Divide the crushed biscuits between four 150 ml (¼ pint) ramekins and press down to line the bottom. Spoon half the yogurt over the biscuit crumbs. Layer with the sliced bananas and the rest of the yogurt.
2 Smooth the tops and sprinkle with demerara sugar. Place the ramekins under a preheated hot grill and cook for 1–2 minutes until the sugar caramelizes – don't leave them any longer or the yogurt will overheat.
3 Leave the banana brûlées to cool, then refrigerate for 1 hour before serving.

75 g (3 oz) digestive biscuits

150 g (5 oz) toffee-flavoured yogurt

2 bananas, sliced

2 tablespoons demerara sugar

Variation
For a slightly less sweet dessert, use Greek yogurt instead of toffee-flavoured.

pear popovers

MAKES 6 • PREP 15 MINS • COOK 20 MINS • CALS PER POPOVER 140 • FAT PER POPOVER 4 G

1 Preheat the oven to gas mark 7/220°C (425°F). Lightly grease a 7.5 cm (3 in) muffin tin, 2.5 cm (1 in) deep.
2 Put the flour and icing sugar into a bowl. Make a well in the centre and break in the egg. Pour in half the milk and mix gently until smooth, then beat in the rest of milk.
3 Pour a little oil into each muffin compartment and place the tin in the oven until really hot. Pour in the batter and put the sliced pears on top. Bake for 20 minutes until golden and risen. Dust with icing sugar and serve, with a dollop of Greek yogurt if desired.

75 g (3 oz) plain flour, sifted

2 tablespoons icing sugar, plus extra for dusting

1 egg

125 ml (4 fl oz) semi-skimmed milk

1 tablespoon olive oil

2 ripe pears, peeled, cored and thinly sliced

Variation
If you prefer, use apples instead of pears for the popovers.

fruity jelly

SERVES 4 • PREP 15 MINS • COOK NONE • CALS PER PORTION 200 • FAT PER PORTION 2 G

1 Break the jelly cubes into pieces and place in a large bowl. Add 250 ml (8 fl oz) boiling water and stir to dissolve. Add 250 ml (8 fl oz) ice-cold water and stir well. Allow to cool.
2 Fill four sturdy glasses with the fruit pieces, ensuring they are tightly packed. Pour over the jelly mix and allow the jelly to set overnight in the fridge.

2 x 135 g (4½ oz) packets lemon jelly

450 g (1 lb) fresh fruit pieces, such as mango, kiwi fruit and seedless grapes

Tips
You need to use the jelly cube type of packet jelly for this recipe. You can find pieces of fresh fruit in the fresh salad bar of large supermarkets.

carrot cake

SERVES 10 • PREP 20 MINS • COOK 50 MINS • CALS PER PORTION 390 • FAT PER PORTION 20 G

1 Preheat the oven to gas mark 4/180°C (350°F).
2 Place all the cake ingredients, except the carrots, in a bowl and beat until smooth. Add the grated carrots and blend very briefly.
3 Pour into a greased 450 g (1 lb) loaf tin and bake for about 50 minutes, until a skewer inserted into the centre comes out clean. Leave to cool in the tin for 5 minutes, then remove to a wire rack.
4 Meanwhile, mix together the ingredients for the icing in a bowl. When the cake is cool, spread the icing over the top.

4 tablespoons sunflower oil

125 g (4 oz) soft brown sugar

½ teaspoon salt

2 eggs

400 g (14 oz) self-raising flour

150 ml (¼ pint) milk

1 teaspoon ground cinnamon

¼ teaspoon ground mixed spice

2 large carrots, peeled and grated

For the icing:

75 g (3 oz) cream cheese

50 g (2 oz) icing sugar

¼ teaspoon ground cinnamon

squeeze of lemon juice

chocolate fridge cake

SERVES 10–12 • PREP 20 MINS, PLUS CHILLING • COOK 5–10 MINS • CALS PER PORTION 470–395 •
FAT PER PORTION 31–26 G

225 g (8 oz) plain chocolate,
broken into small pieces

50 g (2 oz) butter

150 ml (¼ pint) double cream

225 g (8 oz) digestive biscuits,
roughly broken

125 g (4 oz) nuts, chopped

200 g (7 oz) tub naturally
coloured glacé cherries

cocoa powder, for dusting

1 Melt the chocolate and butter in a large heatproof bowl set over
a saucepan of barely simmering water. Stir to mix occasionally,
ensuring the bowl doesn't touch the water. When the chocolate
has melted, remove from the heat and allow to cool.
2 In a bowl, lightly whip the double cream. Fold in the melted
chocolate, the broken biscuits, chopped nuts and the cherries.
3 Spoon the mixture into a lightly greased 20.5 cm (8 in) round
loose-bottomed cake tin, cover with clear film and chill for at
least 4 hours.
4 To serve, dust the top with cocoa powder and cut into wedges.